UNIVERSAL **GUIDELINE** FOR HUMAN HEALTH

RECOMMENDATIONS FOR PLANT-BASED NUTRITION, PHYSICAL ACTIVITY, SLEEP, STRESS MANAGEMENT, AND SUPPORT SYSTEMS

MARGARITA RESTREPO & MICHELE NASINI

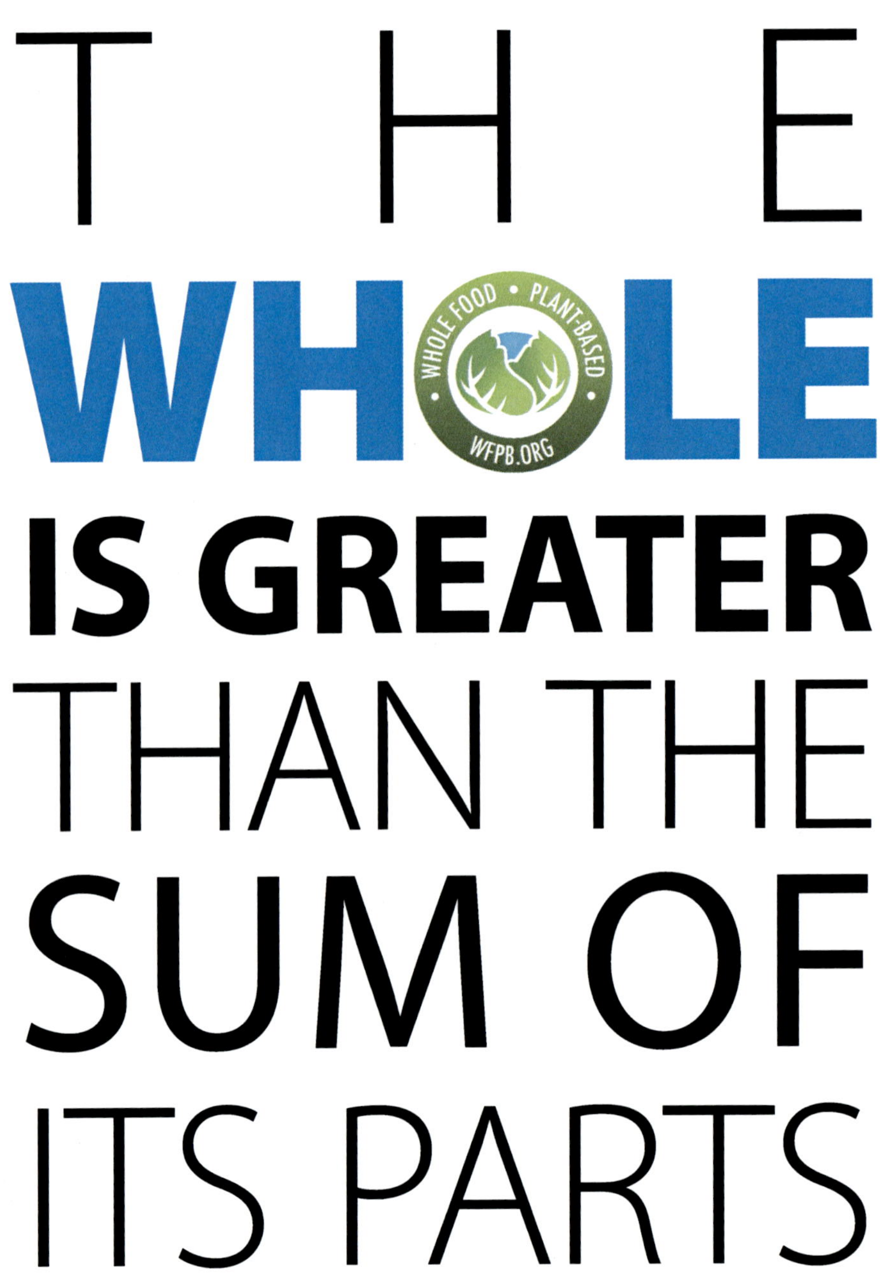
THE
WHOLE
WHOLE FOOD • PLANT-BASED
WFPB.ORG
IS GREATER
THAN THE
SUM OF
ITS PARTS

The Universal Guideline for Human Health | Second Edition
First Published in 2018, Copyright @ 2024, Naked Earth OU
Release Date: July 2024
Publisher and Distributor: Naked Earth OU
Authors: Margarita Restrepo, Michele Nasini

###

This document has no private or corporate sponsorship,
nor any religious, economic, political, academic, or corporate bias.

The Universal Guideline is independently developed by **The Whole Food, Plant-based Initiative (WFPB ORG)** and sponsored by the **International Association of Reversive Medicine** and **Naked Food Magazine**.

###

Disclaimer: *The information and advice herein are not intended for use in, or as a substitute for, the diagnosis or treatment of any health or physical condition or as a substitute for a physician-patient relationship, which has been established by an in-person evaluation of a patient. Do not change your diet if you are ill or on medication without the advice of a qualified healthcare professional such as your physician.*

ABOUT THIS GUIDELINE

The **Universal Guideline for Human Health,** or Part One, is an essential resource for individuals, families, communities and anyone seeking to promote health and prevent disease. It provides advice on how to achieve optimum health as well as what to eat and drink to meet nutrient needs through plant-based nutrition and lifestyle changes. The guideline provides detailed guidance focused on preventing diet-related chronic diseases such as **heart disease, dementia, obesity, type 2 diabetes, nephritis and cancer** through a comprehensive approach (rather than a partial or isolated one) to health and wellbeing. It is suitable for health professionals and policymakers as they design and implement health, food and/or nutrition programs that provide information to the general public. The current edition focuses on lifestyle changes and plant-based nutrition recommendations using a lifespan approach for all age groups.

Grounded in the most current scientific evidence available today, this **Universal Guideline for Human Health** covers the main pillars of good health treating it in a coherent and cohesive manner where the physical, emotional, mental and spiritual bodies of an individual are addressed together as a whole. It includes in-depth information on how to follow a **Whole Approach to Health** and the **New Health Pyramid** based on positive lifestyle habits. It also provides a comprehensive **Food List**, as well as a list of **Foods to Avoid**, **Plant-Based Substitutions for Common Foods**, advice on **How to Build a Meal**, and how to do **Meal Planning**. For the first time, a Guideline designed for public health includes advice on how to perform basic **Physical Training** (and features a Sample Program for Health and Longevity), as well as **Lifestyle Habits to Improve Sleep**, to **Reduce Stress** and to promote health and wellbeing through the practice of **Meditation**.

In the upcoming Part Two of the Universal Guideline, we focus on the solutions and recommendations for environmental health. There is substantial scientific evidence that links human health with **food, air, water and soil quality**, which today is constantly threatened by **geoengineering, genetic modification, chemical treatments, deforestation, and animal agriculture**. We also address the problems with the **food, medical and pharmaceutical industries** which are controlled by private corporations to create a system of dependency, unhealth, and dis-ease for the global population.

Margarita Restrepo
Founder, The Whole Food, Plant-based Initiative (WFPB.ORG)
Founder and President, International Association of Reversive Medicine™
Founder and Editor-in-Chief, Naked Food Magazine

ABOUT THE AUTHORS

Margarita Restrepo

Margarita Restrepo is a **Naturopath** and avid whole food, plant-based and vegan chef. She owns **Naked Earth**, an independent publishing company that provides awakening content all over the world. Margarita is the founder and editor-in-chief of the award-winning publication **Naked Food magazine**, the founder and pioneer of **Reversive Medicine**, and the founder of **The Whole Food, Plant-based Initiative, WFPB ORG**.

She is the author of the evidence-based **4-Body Cancer Protocol** and the author of five whole food, plant-based and vegan **Culinary Medicine** cookbooks. She is certified in **Cellular Biology** as well as **Cognitive Health** from **Harvard University**, **Virology and Microbiology** from **Columbia University**, and **Plant-based Nutrition** from **Cornell**. Though most of her practice is focused on cancer reversal, through fasting and dietary interventions she coaches patients on weight loss and the reversal of other chronic metabolic conditions such as obesity, diabetes, and heart disease. She also practices herbal medicine, foraging, and permaculture.

Michele Nasini

Michele Nasini is a professional **Fitness Coach** certified in **Strength and Conditioning Training** from the prestigious **Setanta College** in Ireland. He is the founder of **MN Athletics** and the owner of **Cruinn Gym**. He is a **Weightlifting** and **Calisthenics** athlete as well as a former competitive swimmer. Michele is a researcher in the fields of esoterism, occultism, and symbolism and a pioneer in the application of these findings onto the biology and essence of the human body.

Michele is a published author and partner of **Naked Earth**, an independent publishing company that provides awakening content all over the world. Through his coaching practice and publications, he strives to improve health and wellbeing through **physical exercise** and **body awareness**.

ABOUT WFPB.ORG

WFPB.ORG is the **Whole Food, Plant-based Initiative** that empowers conscious and comprehensive health for humans and planet through a plant-based lifestyle. WFPB addresses human dis-ease as an imbalance in its own environment or **cellular terrain**. Its approach is based in the **symbiotic interconnection that exists in nature** and its application to lifestyle and environment as influencing factors for human health. WFPB promotes **self-care** instead of disease-care and educates on the most basic, natural, and evidence-based ways of healing. WFPB promotes a **cohesive (whole)** practice where **physical, emotional, mental,** and **spiritual** factors encompass a whole person and provide benefits toward a healthier and more awakened self.

CERTIFIED SEAL OF APPROVAL

WFPB.ORG **administers the "WFPB Certified" seal**, an easy-to-recognize trademarked symbol for **whole, plant-based brands, products, services, professionals, and businesses.** The seal helps consumers navigate through the sea of available products on the market by identifying those that comply with the standard consumers expect. Please visit **wfpb.org/certification** to learn more.

✓ No Animal Products or Byproducts
✓ No Insect Products or Byproducts
✓ No Cultured or Cell-based meats
✓ No Processed Ingredients
✓ No Synthetic Ingredients
✓ No Lab-made Substances
✓ No Chemicals, Colorants, or Toxins
✓ No Junk or Fillers

The WFPB™ (whole food, plant-based) symbol ensures that brands/products/services:

- Help prevent, reverse, and heal human disease
- Aid in the lowering of death and mortality due to preventable causes
- Lower the global statistics of early morbidity due to diet and nutrition
- Reduce the cost of healthcare for individuals and their communities
- Help individuals make positive lifestyle changes and contribute to their wellbeing
- Provide an ideal option for children's health and early development including pregnancy
- Increase the availability of high-quality options for the local and global community
- Increase the demand for truly healthy and wholesome products and services
- Improve the understanding of coherent lifestyle choices
- Help increase soil health and planetary preservation
- Decrease the demand and consumption of genetically engineered organisms (GMO)
- Decrease industrialized farming practices

AVAILABLE COACHING

Nutritional Intervention Coaching for Optimum Health, Weight Loss, Disease Reversal and Prevention

Through nutritional interventions and lifestyle changes, WFPB offers personalized health assessments and guided meal planning for individuals and groups. Programs are suitable to individuals with health conditions as well as to those who wish to maintain or improve their wellbeing. Each plan is made according to an individual's goals and needs with ongoing guidance and assistance through the process.

Please contact LifestyleChanges@wfpb.org for an assessment or further information.

Physical Training Coaching for Health, Longevity, and Weight Loss

Considering factors like body type, physical shape and training experience is key to creating a personalized program that can meet the goals and necessities of each person. WFPB offers individual assessments and consultations with a trained professional who can build and provide a customized training program. Programs are made according to an individual's goals and needs with ongoing guidance and assistance throughout the process.

Please contact PhysicalTraining@wfpb.org for an assessment or further information.

TABLE OF CONTENTS

WHOLE FOOD • PLANT-BASED •
WFPB.ORG

HUMAN AND PLANETARY HEALTH: MAKING THE CONNECTION

Human and environmental health are dependent on one another. What we breathe, drink and consume greatly influences our personal health, the economic health of our countries, and the health of the planet we all share.

The environment affects the health and wellbeing of every living being that inhabits it, including humans.

Though the literature on sustainable diets has grown substantially in the past decade,[1 2 3 4] and the concept has been expanded to the economic, ethical, and cultural aspects of food consumption,[5] consistent health analyses of commonly proposed diets are scarce.[6] An approach that is cohesively sustainable, healthy, and conscious for humans, animals and the planet hasn't been considered until now. Neither has one that proposes a comprehensive approach to treat human health and wellbeing considering all the aspects of the human experience such as its physical aspect, plus mental, emotional and spiritual are non-existent.

Because of this, we propose a comprehensive (whole) approach based on a sustainable health structure[7] that combines a plant-based nutritional structure, physical activity, sleep, stress reduction and support systems as the proven core and most reliable basis for optimum health for humans.

WHY PLANT-BASED?

a. Global Health Burden

Imbalanced diets low in fruits, vegetables, nuts, and whole grains, and high in red and processed meat are responsible for the greatest health burden worldwide.[8 9] In addition to imbalanced diets, high consumption of red and processed meat and low consumption of fruits and vegetables are important diet-related risk factors contributing to substantial early mortality in most regions.

- Seven of the top ten causes of death worldwide are due to preventable diseases. Ischemic heart disease and stroke are the world's biggest killers, accounting for a combined 15.2 million deaths in 2016. These diseases have remained the leading causes of death globally in the last 15 years.
- Other leading causes include chronic obstructive pulmonary disease which claimed 3.0 million lives in 2016, while lung cancer, along with trachea and bronchus cancers, caused 1.7 million deaths.
- Diabetes killed 1.6 million people in 2016, up from less than 1 million in 2000.
- Deaths due to dementia more than doubled between 2000 and 2016, making it the 5th leading cause of global deaths in 2016 compared to 14th in 2000.[10]

These dietary health risks are expected to worsen[11] by increasing the human, social, and economic health burden from chronic diseases associated with high body weight and unhealthy diets.[12]

b. Global Economic Burden

Rates of these chronic, diet-related diseases continue to rise, and they come not only with increased health risks, but also at high health cost.

- In 2014, more than 2.1 billion people—nearly 30% of the global population—were overweight or obese and 5% of the deaths worldwide were attributable to obesity.[13] In 2014 the global economic impact of obesity[14 15 16 17 18 19 20 21] was estimated to be US $2.0 trillion or 2.8% of the global gross domestic product (GDP).[22]
- The global cost of diabetes is now $825 billion per year.[23 24 25] The total economic loss due to cardiovascular disease in low- and middle-income countries was estimated to amount to $3.7 trillion (2010) between 2011 and 2015.[26 27]
- In the United States alone, medical costs linked to obesity are estimated to be $147 billion. In 2012, the total estimated cost of diagnosed diabetes was $245 billion, including $176 billion in direct medical costs and $69 billion in decreased productivity.

c. Planetary Burden

Meat production contributes disproportionately to the planetary burden, in part because feeding grain to livestock to produce meat—instead of feeding grain directly to humans—involves a large energy loss, making animal agriculture more resource-intensive than other forms of food production.

- Pollution: The proliferation of factory-style animal agriculture creates environmental and public health concerns, including pollution from the high concentration of animal wastes and the extensive use of antibiotics, which compromise their effectiveness in medical use.
- Corporate Lead: Global food production is mainly controlled by private corporations.
- Unsustainability: Global food production generates food deserts, food scarcity, and food waste.
- Disease: At the consumption end, animal-based food is implicated in many of the chronic degenerative diseases that afflict industrial and newly industrializing societies, particularly cardiovascular disease and cancer.
- Toxicity: The pesticides used heavily in industrial agriculture are associated with elevated cancer risks for workers and consumers and are coming under greater scrutiny for their links to endocrine disruption and reproductive dysfunction.[28]
- Deforestation: Large-scale animal agriculture is the leading cause of deforestation in the Amazon Rainforest,[29] and the growth of this unsustainable trade is created by consumer demand. As the demand for meat rises worldwide, so must the production of meat. Since 1978 over 750,000 square kilometers (289,000 square miles) of Amazon rainforest have been destroyed across Brazil, Peru, Colombia, Bolivia, Venezuela, Suriname, Guyana, and French Guiana.

Furthermore, about 800 million people are still suffering from hunger due to poverty and poorly developed food systems.[30] In the absence of dedicated strategies or changes in demand, many of these human, economic, and

environmental impacts are expected to intensify as demand for meat and dairy increases and the global population grows from 7 billion to a predicted 10 billion in the next 30 years.[31]

Beyond animal agriculture, other factors that are highly affecting human health include food, air, water and soil quality, which today is constantly threatened by geoengineering, genetic modification, and chemical treatments.

All of the above conditions threaten environmental resilience and create a system of corporate and medical dependency, general unhealth, and biological dis-ease for the global population that continues to benefit corporations, medical and pharmaceutical industries and governmental organizations instead of the public.

THE WHOLE APPROACH TO HEALTH

In 2005, Meyer-Abich[32] published a comprehensive position paper "to explain how the philosophy of nutrition is *part* of the philosophy of health" and "to show that this link allows practical solutions for equity and sustainability" (p. 738).[33] In fact, in addition to diet, a healthy model should be considered from a more integral perspective that considers physical exercise and well-being as including interconnectedness with other living beings of the natural and social environment as a whole.

Meyer-Abich concluded his article by writing, "We are not individually healthy, but we are so in togetherness, even with animals and plants.[34] Comprehensive nutrition science has physical, social and environmental attributes". He also wrote that "Nutrition and health are central dimensions of the way of life, which has been known since antiquity as *diaita*" and "The present-day constriction of this broad meaning to the term "diet" covers only the aspects of eating and drinking— and is a symptom of the reductionism of our age".[35]

As the opposite of reductionism, whole-ism asserts that naturally interconnected systems (e.g., physical, biologic, chemical, social, economic, mental, spiritual, and linguistic) should be viewed as wholes and that their functioning cannot be fully understood solely in terms of their component parts.

Studies of health and their solutions for wellbeing should integrate environmental, socioeconomic, and spiritual dimensions to obtain a circumspect view of the sustainability of human life in relation to one-self, the corporate interests involved, the Earth and the food system among others.[36]

a. Nutritional Reductionism

Nutritional reductionism[37] refers to the focus on individual food compounds (e.g., protein, vitamins, antioxidants) as opposed to an integral or whole approach that focuses on food habits and the relationship between diet and health, particularly chronic conditions such as cancer[38] and heart disease.

Reductionism has conquered the modern lifestyle. Food is no longer considered based on its benefits to human health, but based on its macronutrient properties, and therefore, food is either protein, carb or fat. Food has become nothing but its parts, and its only considered by its calories or its chemical properties when in reality, real food does not and should not be analyzed by its parts but by its complete nutritional value. It should not be divided into sub-categories but instead appreciated for its comprehensive benefits.

A plant is able to produce fruit thanks to the environmental conditions that support and surround it. The sun and the process of photosynthesis, the soil, water and oxygen create a specific and ideal terrain (or habitat) to allow its roots to absorb nutrients, the sun to induce chlorophyll and ATP, and the fruit to be produced. This fruit contains a plethora of nutrients, antioxidants, enzymes, molecules, and specific substances that can only be present in it as a whole, because it was produced as a whole, not as individual parts.

The subject of nutrition and health in general, has been treated as individual parts. Nutrition is a wholistic science, whereas medical practice is reductionist, a serious mismatch that causes biased judgment of nutrition.[39] Reductionism is the basis of nutritional research, food and supplement production, and misleading marketing because it targets one individual condition or state, one nutrient, or one particular aspect of the whole.

It is more logical to consider a situation first from a wholistic perspective and to then apply a reductionist approach when necessary to address a particular issue, rather than beginning by studying a particular point and attempting to explain the whole from this part. Unfortunately, research in human nutrition and food science has been conducted primarily based on a bottom-up approach, from the specific to the general, particularly for nutritional recommendations. If diet and health advisories were to acknowledge the biological complexity of nutrition and make greater use of deductive (top down) instead of inductive (bottom up) reasoning, there would be less confusion.[40]

b. Deficiency Mentality

A "deficiency mentality" considers that a disease is caused by a lack of a particular compound, which in turn supports a reductionist paradigm. Some of this thought has grown from diseases such as scurvy that have been treated successfully with vitamin extracts, thus scientists and doctors are trained to find the "magic bullet" to cure a disease, an approach that is not successful in treating modern chronic diseases.

Supplements are a billion-dollar industry. Supplements are, for the most part, synthetic compounds produced in laboratories to attempt to reproduce those compounds that come from nature—and are naturally part of a greater whole. Supplements are one major consequence of the misunderstanding of health and nutrition as it is believed that they are the solutions for a variety of issues, including a bad diet and poor nutrition. Synthetic supplements are not bioavailable and are absorbed by the human body in very low percentages, such as a mere 2%. It would be more appropriate to suggest the consumption of more fruits and vegetables to increase the nutrient consumption from natural sources which the body can absorb 100%. In the pharmaceutical industry, at least 5,000 phytonutrients in

plants have been linked to the *possibility* of decreasing risk of major chronic diseases, therefore, there is great economical interest in continuing a reductionist paradigm that supports it.

Having said that, there are also some types of supplementation that can be useful in specific cases, for example nascent iodine for T4 and T3 thyroid health (*See Iodine*), vitamin B12 for brain health (*See Vitamin B12*), Vitamin D3 in some cases or depending on geographical location (*See Vitamin D),* Probiotics (*See Probiotics),* and some other supplements that may be needed to address a specific of deficiency in particular cases.

c. Whole-ism vs. Reductionism

When it comes to food, it is important to understand what a whole food vs. a processed food is. To most people, the word whole may mean that one may need to eat the entire food or meal, and that a processed food is simply junk food. Though there is some truth to that, the concept goes beyond this and must be clearly understood.

A "processed food" is the result of one or various elements that have been ***extracted*** from their original source. When a single nutrient is extracted from a food **all other essential nutrients that make it an integral or complete food are left out**. This is the case of isolated proteins, for example, where all other nutrients from the original whole food (corn, soy, or peas) such as its fiber, essential fatty-acids, carbohydrates, minerals, and vitamins are left out and only the protein is used. The resulting element is one hundred percent protein, isolated from its original source and because of this is no longer whole.

The same concept can be applied to sugar cane or corn kernels, where only the glucose is extracted to create sugar or corn syrup.

When only the fat is extracted from an olive, an avocado, a seed or from any other plant, it produces oil. The process follows the same model. The end result, meaning the oil, is 100% fat as only the fat has been extracted from its original source. All other nutrients such as fiber, protein, carbohydrates, antioxidants, minerals and vitamins have been left out. The extracted elements are considered single isolated nutrients that for the most part lose their bioavailability or more importantly, behave differently than when naturally contained in their original form.

All processed food is created with the same reductionist model, for example: white flour (extracted wheat compound from whole wheat), white sugar (extracted glucose compound from whole cane tree or beet), corn syrup (extracted glucose compound from corn kernels), oils (extracted fat compound from various plants), isolated proteins (extracted amino acid compound from various foods). Other isolated compounds include chemicals, preservatives, acids, and other artificial elements.

A sustainable nutritional recommendation must make an imperative difference between whole and processed foods to ensure that new nutritional patterns aren't merely slightly better but sustainably appropriate. The most important aspect of this differentiation is the way the body absorbs and integrates nutrients that come from a whole

food or an isolated or processed one. In over 100 studies, the synergistic anti-cancer and antioxidant effects of fruits, vegetables, grains and legumes consumed together are not duplicated with the consumption of isolated pill extracts from the same foods. Also, studies show that eating a variety of whole plant foods increases the positive nutritional benefits above the sum of the individual plant components.

Pills cannot mimic the effects of plant food nutrient synergies:

- Fiber extracts do not provide the same heart disease prevention benefits of fiber-containing plant foods.[41]
- Beta Carotene extracts have been shown to worsen—not improve—lung cancer, while whole plant foods containing beta carotene have been shown to be protective.[42]
- Curcumin extracted from the spice turmeric is not as effective an anti-cancer and anti-inflammation agent as the whole spice.[43]
- Broccoli sprouts have been effective targeting cancer stem cells while broccoli sprout extract has not.[44]
- Resistant starch extracts and enriched foods have not shown the same anti-colon cancer properties as whole resistant-starch-containing plant foods.[45]

THE SUSTAINABLE CHANGE

A whole food, plant-based diet accompanied by lifestyle factors such as sleep, physical activity, stress reduction, and sunshine are the basis of a healthy human body. Human and environmental health is intrinsically connected. As humans are the dominant species on Earth, the environmental health of our planet relies on human actions and behaviors. Conversely, human health depends on the planet's ability to provide adequate resources for humans to thrive such as water, oxygen, soil, food, and other essential nutrients.

The Iceberg (Figure 1) is the graphic depiction of two health ecosystems working as one toward achieving human and planetary sustainability. It is also based on a top-down (wholistic) approach instead of a bottom-up (reductionist) approach to research and well-being.

The basis for environmental health (top structure) describes the phases to achieve education and consciousness levels of health, that when applied to entire communities, creates global impact. The basis for human health (bottom structure) describes the configuration of a well-planned whole food, plant-based lifestyle that involves a state of complete physical, mental, and social well-being, and not merely the **absence of disease.**

The entire ecosystem can be achieved by making plant-based foods and materials more available, accessible, and affordable in place of unhealthy and unsustainable alternatives, improving information and food marketing, investing in unbiased public health information and sustainability education such as this Universal Guideline, using health care services to deliver proper dietary advice and nutritional interventions, and implementing these health guidelines in educational institutions around the world.

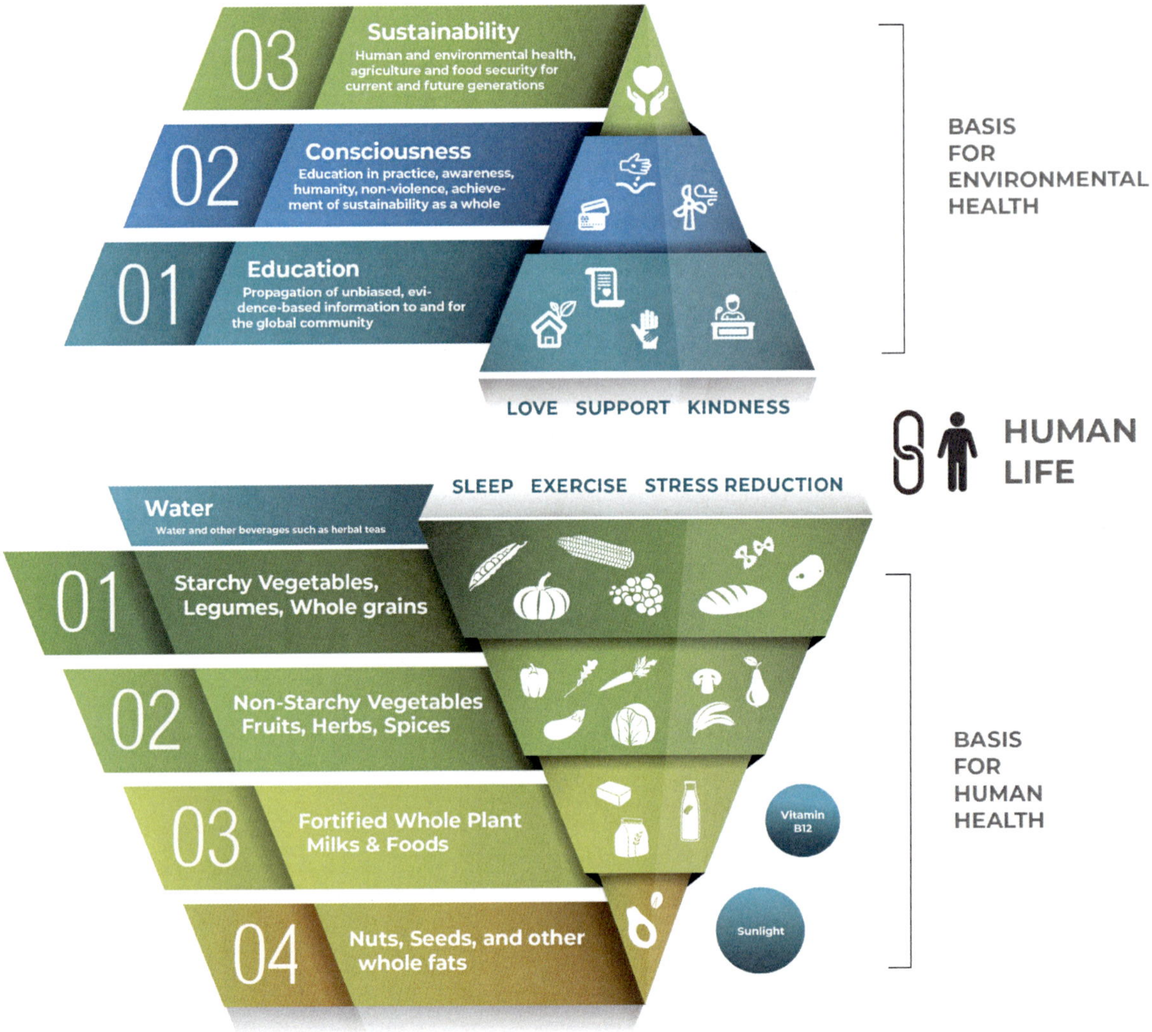

03 Sustainability
Human and environmental health, agriculture and food security for current and future generations

02 Consciousness
Education in practice, awareness, humanity, non-violence, achievement of sustainability as a whole

01 Education
Propagation of unbiased, evidence-based information to and for the global community

LOVE SUPPORT KINDNESS

BASIS FOR ENVIRONMENTAL HEALTH

HUMAN LIFE

SLEEP EXERCISE STRESS REDUCTION

Water
Water and other beverages such as herbal teas

01 Starchy Vegetables, Legumes, Whole grains

02 Non-Starchy Vegetables Fruits, Herbs, Spices

03 Fortified Whole Plant Milks & Foods

04 Nuts, Seeds, and other whole fats

Vitamin B12

Sunlight

BASIS FOR HUMAN HEALTH

{Figure 1: Icebergs harbor their own complex ecosystems, and they shape the ecosystems through which they pass. As humans, we have the power of building these same ecosystems and crafting ideal environments that establish health and sustainability on a global scale}.

The ability to make an educated choice is the ultimate game-changer; therefore, educated consumers have the power to create demand for the products and services they want. By promoting truly conscious consumer and commercial goods and services in manufacturing, transportation, agriculture, and household, consumer industries can pave the way to a financially strong and sustainable socio-economic future.

Human and Planetary Health Outcomes

Education:

- **Empowerment.**
  Education is the key to creating an educated society that chooses consciously instead of following marketing trends that benefit big corporations, big cancer, big pharma and/or other unsustainable industries.
- **Market Demand.**
  Consumers have the power to create demand for the products and services that best fit their needs.
- **Clean Products.**
  Creating demand for truly healthful, non-toxic, and non-polluting processes and goods in agriculture and manufacturing for a more conscious consumer.

Consciousness:

- **Awarencss.**
  The iceberg represents the above and below from a wholistic perspective. Nourishing the body and cellular terrain on the inside and the conscious aspect of our actions on the outside.
- **Non-Violence.**
  Animals produced for human consumption are routinely abused, used and utilized for nutritional purposes, however, as explained in this guideline, animals eat plants to acquire the nutrients they need, and so can humans. A WFPB lifestyle is non-violent, kind, and conscious, as it does not require any animal use. Furthermore, it can help reduce environmental degradation by drastically reducing water and land use, deforestation, water and air pollution and biodiversity loss.
- **Global Change.**
  By diminishing the demand for animal products, we can effectively reduce land use, and improve the health of our waterways and oceans. All this can improve global health like no other action can.

Sustainability:

- **Health.**
  A plant-based lifestyle creates sustainable demand for foods that prevent and/or reverse acute, chronic, and degenerative conditions that are the most common causes of disease and death globally.
- **Regenerative Agriculture.**
  This demand empowers farmers to position themselves at the top of the market instead of the bottom while creating more natural and chemical free environments for crops and biodiversity. Regenerative agriculture is also one positive way to achieve self-sufficiency and independence from the corporate-controlled system.

- **Food Security.**
  By demanding organic crops produced through conscious and regenerative agriculture and permaculture (toxic chemical and GMO-free practices) we can build systems that are profitable and beneficial for all.

Global Impacts

a. Health Impacts by 2050[46]

- Transitioning toward a plant-based diet could reduce global mortality by 6–10% by the year 2050.
- The global adoption of this type of dietary guideline based on a plant-based diet (no red meat, poultry, fish, dairy, or eggs), would result in **8.1 million avoided deaths** (CI, 7.8–8.5 million) and **129 million life years saved** (CI, 125–133 million).
- About 45–47% of all avoided deaths are from reduced coronary heart disease (CHD), 26% from stroke, 16–18% from cancer, and 10–12% from type-2 diabetes mellitus.

Global Regional breakdown

The greatest number of avoided deaths occurs in developing countries, in particular in East Asia (31–35%) and South Asia (15–19%).

- Reducing red meat consumption is the change that has the most positive effect on health in East Asia (78–82%), Western high- and middle-income countries (64–71%; 58–65%), and Latin America (42–48%).
- Increasing fruit and vegetable consumption is responsible for the majority of avoided deaths in the least developed regions (South Asia, 75–83%; Sub-Saharan Africa, 72–84%).
- Reduced energy intake and the resulting fewer people overweight and obese are particularly important in the Eastern Mediterranean (41–79%), Latin America (32–48%), and Western high- and middle-income countries (29–40%; 20–33%).

b. Economic Impacts by 2050

The monetized value associated with diet-related changes in mortality amounts to 21 trillion (or 10^{12}) US dollars per year ($21 trillion) in 2050 with a range of $10–31 trillion. In terms of percentage of expected global GDP in 2050, these values amount to 13% (6–20%).

UNIVERSAL GUIDELINE FOR HUMAN HEALTH

The basic needs for human life and its survival include water, air, and sunlight. Humans can survive in water-only environments for weeks and water-only consumption (also called water fasting) is strongly recommended to rebalance, regenerate, detoxify, and rebuild cells, organs, and essential functions. (See *Fasting*).

Dis-ease can in most cases be addressed and halted with the complete absence of food and the ingestion of water only. Fasting is primarily a rest of the organism.[47] Rest gives all the organs an opportunity to repair the damaged structures, and there is no condition of disease in which rest of vital organs is not a benefit to the whole organism. By affording the organs of the body a rest, fasting grows and improves the body's power of digestion and assimilation. It does this by withholding raw materials, stopping the inflow of decomposition-poisons and the consumption of a problem-causing nutritive *excess*.[48] It promotes the removal of circulating and deposited toxins, the normalization of blood chemistry, and cellular and tissue regeneration.

Subsequently, if one of the best possible scenarios for the body is to give it a rest, then the consumption of any other nutrients in the form of food must be carefully thought out and food should be the closest to its natural state, in its whole form, as possible. Therefore, the consumption of fruits and vegetables in their raw form, sprouts, nuts and seeds as well as some cooked foods is ideal.

For all aspects of health, we present the main five pillars for a comprehensive, cohesive and wholistic approach which include nutrition, physical activity, sleep, stress reduction, and support systems.

1. NUTRITION

Only a low-fat, whole food, plant-based dietary pattern has been clearly demonstrated to reduce the risk of many chronic diseases for decades[49] and has been associated with improved wellbeing in all aspects of human health such as lowering overall and ischemic heart disease mortality;[50] [51] supporting sustainable weight management;[52] reducing medication needs;[53] [54] [55] lowering the risk for most chronic diseases;[56] [57] decreasing the incidence and severity of high-risk conditions, including obesity,[58] [59] [60] [61] [62] [63] [64] hypertension,[65] [66] [67] hyperlipidemia,[68] and hyperglycemia;[69] mortality,[70] [71] [72] [73] [74] cancer,[75] and even reversing advanced coronary artery disease[76] [77] [78] [79] [80] [81] [82] [83] [84] [85] and type 2 diabetes.[86] [87] [88]

Fruits and vegetables are the healthiest and most beneficial source of antioxidants, including Beta-carotene, vitamin C, vitamin E, and selenium. Many of these compounds scavenge reactive oxygen species, including free radicals, which increase oxidative stress and have been associated with aging, CHD, diabetes, cancer, arthritis, and other chronic diseases as well as Alzheimer's and Parkinson's disease.[89] [90] [91] [92] [93] [94] [95] [96]

Chronic disease determinants or anthropogens (anthropogenic effects, processes, objects, or materials derived from human activities), have varying levels of potency depending on a range of factors such as genes, environment, and exposure. Although each may impact independently in the development of chronic disease, findings have suggested it is more realistic to think of *interactions* as a whole or integral process taking place in a living organism, both within and between determinant factors, instead of a simple linear approach (Hamed, 2009). Just like isolating nutrients from foods ignores the interactive relationship of nutrients found in whole meal patterns (see *Whole-ism vs. Reductionism*), considering inactivity, sleep, or social factors in the absence of nutrition provides only part of the etiological answer to disease manifestation. The interactions between determinants may be hidden below the surface, like an iceberg, but is a most important aspect of a modern Lifestyle Medicine approach to chronic diseases and conditions.[97]

A. NUTRITIONAL RECOMMENDATIONS

A healthful *and* sustainable nutrition pattern is low in fat and is based on plant-based starches (beans, whole rice, corn, potatoes, quinoa) with the addition of vegetables, fruits, legumes, seeds and nuts.[98] [99]

Scientific documentation of what most people have eaten over at least the past 13,000 years concludes that throughout human history once thriving populations including the Japanese,[100] Chinese,[101] [102] [103] and other Asians eating sweet potatoes, buckwheat, and/or rice; Incas[104] in South America eating potatoes; Mayas[105] [106] and Aztecs[107] [108] [109] in Central America eating corn; and Egyptians[110] [111] in the Middle East eating wheat; have obtained the bulk of their calories from plant starches.

As described in this Universal Guideline, a healthful nutritional pattern maximizes consumption of nutrient-dense plant foods while avoiding processed foods, added sugars, added oils, and all animal-derived foods (including dairy products and eggs).[112]

B. DAILY FOOD SERVING SUGGESTION

Three to six (3-6) whole food, plant-based meals per day with the following structure:

1. Base of Plant-based Starches:

Starchy Vegetables, Whole Grains, and *Legumes* as the main calorie sources.

2. Add Quantities as Desired (No limit): *Non-Starchy Vegetables, Leafy Greens and Cruciferous Vegetables; Fruit, Herbs, Spices,* and *Water.*

3. Add Daily (Limit Depending on Energy needs and health status): *Nuts* and *Seeds.*

C. FOOD GROUPS

PLANT STARCHES: Starchy Vegetables, Whole grains, and Legumes (3-6 Servings Daily)

a. Starchy Vegetables

- Acorn Squash*
- Banana Squash*
- Butternut Squash*
- Corn
- Hubbard Squash*
- Jerusalem Artichoke
- Jicama
- Potato
- Pumpkin
- Pumpkin Sprouts
- Purple Potato
- Spaghetti Squash*
- Squash*
- Sweet Potato
- Taro
- Yam
- Yucca (Cassava)

* Actually a fruit, but treated as a vegetable from a culinary perspective

. Whole Grains

- Amaranth
- Barley
- Brown Rice
- Buckwheat
- Bulgur
- Kamut
- Kañiwa
- Millet
- Oats
- Quinoa
- Rye
- Sorghum
- Spelt
- Teff
- Triticale
- Wheat Sprouts
- Whole Wheat
- Wild Rice

c. Legumes

- Alfalfa Sprouts
- Adzuki Beans
- Bean Sprouts
- Black Beans
- Black-Eyed Peas
- Bola Roja Beans
- Borlotti Beans
- Broad Beans
- Cranberry Beans
- Chickpeas/Garbanzos
- Chickpea Sprouts
- Clover
- Clover Sprouts
- Northern Beans
- Kidney Beans
- Lentils
- Lentil Sprouts
- Lima /Butter Beans
- Lupin Beans
- Miso
- Mung Beans
- Mung Bean Sprouts
- Navy Beans
- Peas
- Pea Sprouts
- Split Peas
- Tempeh
- Pink Beans
- Pinto Beans
- Scarlet Runner Bean
- Small Red Beans
- Soybeans
- Soybean Sprouts
- Peanut

d. Non-Starchy, Leafy Greens, and Cruciferous Vegetables

- Artichoke
- Arugula (Rocket)
- Asparagus
- Beet
- Beet Greens
- Bok Choy
- Broccoli (all varieties)
- Broccoli Sprouts
- Brussels Sprouts
- Cabbage (all varieties)
- Carrot
- Cauliflower (all varieties)
- Celeriac
- Celery
- Chard
- Chinese Cabbage/Napa Cabbage
- Chinese Greens
- Choy Sum (Flowering cabbage)
- Collard Greens
- Collards
- Cucumber*
- Daikon
- Dandelion Greens
- Eggplant*
- Endive
- Ethiopian Mustard
- Field Pepper weed
- Frisée
- Garden Cress
- Garlic
- Gem Squash
- Ginger
- Green Beans
- Horseradish
- Kale
- Kale Sprouts
- Kohlrabi
- Komatsuna
- Land Cress
- Lettuce
- Maca
- Mizuna
- Mustard Greens
- Mustard Sprouts
- Napa Cabbage
- Okra
- Onions (all varieties)
- Onion Sprouts
- Parsley
- Parsnip
- Patty Pan Squash*
- Radicchio
- Radish
- Radish Sprouts
- Rutabaga (Swede)
- Savoy cabbage
- Spinach
- Tat Soi/Rosette Bok Choy
- Tomato*
- Turnip
- Turnip Greens
- Wasabi
- Water Chestnut
- Watercress
- Wheatgrass
- White Radish
- Zucchini*
- All edible varieties of Fungi/Mushrooms**

* Actually, a fruit, but treated as a vegetable from a culinary perspective

** Actually, a fungus, not a plant

Note: Careful guidance should be provided to patients on warfarin to establish a stable, consistent intake to avoid variations in the efficacy of anticoagulation with the consumption of green leafy vegetables.

e. Fruit (At least 2-4 Servings daily)

- Apple
- Apricot
- Avocado
- Banana
- Breadfruit
- Bilberry
- Blackberry
- Blackcurrant
- Blueberry
- Cantaloupe
- Cherry
- Cherimoya
- Clementine
- Date
- Damson
- Dragon fruit
- Durian
- Elderberry
- Feijoa
- Gooseberry
- Grape
- Grapefruit
- Guava
- Honeydew Melon
- Huckleberry
- Jackfruit
- Kiwifruit
- Kumquat
- Lemon
- Lime
- Lychee
- Mamoncillo
- Mandarin
- Mango
- Melon
- Nectarine
- Orange
- Peach
- Pear
- Pitaya
- Physalis/Tomatillo
- Plum/Prune (dried plum)
- Pineapple
- Pomegranate
- Pomelo
- Purple Mangosteen
- Raisin
- Raspberry
- Rambutan
- Rock Melon
- Star Fruit/Carambola
- Strawberry
- Tangerine
- Watermelon
- All dried fruits

Notes:

Avocado:

For healthy individuals with a cholesterol level of 150 and LDL of 80 or under (without cholesterol-lowering drugs), and without cardiovascular disease *and/or* another condition that requires severe fat restriction, ¼ avocado a day is acceptable as part of any recipe or dish.

Dried Fruits

- Eat moderately. In small quantities, dates, figs, cranberries, molasses, or maple syrup are appropriate as sweetener substitutes for culinary purposes.
- Consume only oil-free and sugar-free varieties.
- Whole dried fruits are high in fiber and contribute significantly to nutrient intake.

f. Spices and Herbs

- Anise
- Basil
- Bay Leaves
- Caraway
- Cardamom
- Cayenne Pepper
- Chamomile
- Chili
- Cilantro
- Cinnamon
- Cloves
- Coriander
- Cumin
- Dill
- Fennel
- Fenugreek
- Garlic
- Ginger
- Lavender
- Lemongrass
- Marjoram
- Mint
- Mustard Seeds (brown, white, black)
- Nettles
- Nutmeg
- Oregano
- Paprika
- Parsley
- Peppermint
- Poppy Seeds
- Rosemary
- Saffron
- Sage
- Savory
- Tarragon
- Thyme
- Turmeric
- Vanilla

g. Nuts [1 serving maximum daily]

Serving Size: ¼ cup (2 ounces)

- Almond
- Beech
- Brazil Nut
- Cashew
- Chestnut
- Coconut***
- Hazelnut
- Macadamia
- Pine Nut/Pignoli
- Pistachio
- Walnut

*** Actually, a drupe, but treated as a nut from a culinary perspective

Notes:

- **For Health and Prevention:** Within the recommended guideline, incorporation of nuts into a healthy dietary pattern has been associated with improvement in atherosclerotic cardiovascular disease risk factors.[113] Nut consumption decreases risk of Type 2 Diabetes Mellitus.[114] [115] [116] [117] [118] [119]
- **For Weight Loss:** Use sparingly when trying to lose weight or to avoid excess calorie consumption.
- **For Disease Reversal:** For Individuals with a condition that requires severe fat restriction, nuts and nut butters should be avoided. Chestnuts are acceptable.

h. Seeds [1 serving daily]

Serving Size: 1-2 tablespoons of ground flax or chia seeds

- Chia
- Flax
- Hemp
- Pumpkin
- Sesame
- Sunflower

Notes:

Whole flax seeds must be ground just before consuming, as they are not digestible whole.

h. Fermented foods and Probiotics [Add daily]

Probiotics, the microorganisms found in fermented foods, are known to up-regulate production of T and dendritic cells that have the potential to suppress inflammation.[120] Probiotics are thought to reduce cholesterol by disrupting bile acids, using cholesterol for nourishment, and/or incorporating cholesterol into the cell wall of the probiotic bacteria.[121] [122]

- Probiotic supplementation has been shown beneficial on biomarkers of inflammation, oxidative stress and pregnancy outcomes,[123] depression,[124] rheumatoid arthritis,[125] and gestational diabetes.[126]

- The efficacy of probiotics is enhanced when taken in the form of fermented food rather than as probiotics alone.[127]

- Kimchi (fermented cabbage) has long been touted for its medicinal properties and is rich in dietary fiber, vitamin C, β-carotene, β-sitosterol, and minerals.[128]

i. Seaweed

Seaweed includes a variety of algae that are excellent sources of dietary fiber and Omega-3, as well as antioxidants and other compounds that are beneficial for CV health. Compounds in seaweed (e.g., alginates, fucoxanthin, fucoidan) exhibit anti-obesity and cholesterol-lowering properties, in part by promoting satiety.[129]

- Spirulina: A recent meta-analysis suggests that Spirulina, a filamentous, spiral-shaped, water blue-green microalgae (Cyanobacterium), has cholesterol-lowering properties.[130]

j. Water and Other Beverages

- **Water:**

  Clean pure, distilled, filtered, or alkaline water should be consumed in unlimited quantities.

- **Tea:**

  Made from organic plants such as green, black, chai, chamomile, earl gray, ginger, hibiscus, jasmine, lemon balm, matcha, almond blossom oolong, peppermint, rooibos, and white tea. Tea contains a significant antioxidant mix including flavonoids and polyphenols may be associated with improved Cardiovascular Disease health and blood lipids based on large observational studies and meta-analyses.[131 132 133 134]

  Note: Loose-leaf tea (free of plastic and paper sachets) without added sugars, sweeteners, or milks and creams (both animal- and plant-based) is recommended.

- **Plant-based milks:**

  Fortified and non-fortified non-dairy plant milk such as rice, nut, soy, or hemp.

- **Blended or pureed vegetable drinks:**

  A combination of fruit and vegetable pureed drinks with an approximate percentage of 70% vegetable, 30% fruit from fresh or frozen whole foods has been found to improve antioxidant capacity and vasoreactivity.[135 136]

  Notes

  - Vegetable juices are mostly recommended for those needing to improve antioxidant status as antioxidant absorption is improved with the removal of the fiber. This can be of value for several conditions and for athletes (e.g., beet juice).
  - Juicing is primarily reserved for situations when daily intake of vegetables and fruits is inadequate.
  - Avoid the addition of sugars (e.g., honey, stevia, other sweeteners) to minimize caloric overconsumption. (see *Added Sugar*)

D. OTHER NUTRITIONAL RECOMMENDATIONS

a. Added Sugar: [Sugar = 0% to <5% maximum of total calories per day]
A plant-based diet provides adequate amounts of calories from naturally occurring sugars. A nutritional pattern void [0%] or limited to <5%[137] [138] of total energy intake coming from added sugars is recommended.

Notes:

- Added sugars refer to the single extracted nutrients from a whole food such as disaccharides (sucrose or table sugar) added to foods and drinks by the manufacturer, cook, or consumer, and sugars naturally present in syrups, commercial fruit juices, fruit juice concentrates, the liquid high fructose corn syrup (HFCS), and any extracted sugars such as brown sugar, stevia, and other non-plant derived sweeteners such as honey. (see *Whole-ism vs. Reductionism*)
- The negative health effects of excess sugar include fat deposition, adiposity, and dental caries[139] [140] in children and adolescents aged ≥2 to ≥18 years,[141] and coronary heart disease (CHD), stroke, and CVD mortality[142] in adults.

b. Added Sodium: [Sodium = Max. 1,500mg per day]
A whole food, plant-based diet provides between 400-600mg of sodium daily from naturally occurring sodium. It is acceptable to add a daily maximum of ½ teaspoon of sea salt or iodized salt, or 1 tablespoon miso, tamari, or soy sauce, which add about 1,000mg of sodium per day. Total milligrams (mg) sodium intake should be a maximum of 1,500mg per day.[143]

Adequate Sodium Intakes (AIs) according to age are:

- 110mg daily for infants 0-6 months
- 370mg daily for infants 7-12 months
- 800mg daily for children ages 1-3
- 1000mg daily for ages 4-8
- 1200mg daily for ages 9-13
- 1500mg daily for ages 14 and older

Notes:

- Foods should be flavored with spices, vegetables, and herbs instead of salt during the cooking process. Salt should be consumed, if at all, by lightly sprinkling it over a served dish or meal.
- There remains limited scientific evidence on sodium intakes below 1500 mg per day for adults, which prevents considering further reductions in the sodium AI.
- The United States dietary guidelines recommend sodium intake to be less than 2,300 mg/day.[144] The UK National Health Service recommends no more than 2,400mg/day.[145]

E. FOODS THAT MAY NEED TO BE LIMITED

a. Fruits such as:

- **Avocado:** Serving size: ¼ avocado a day as part of any recipe or dish. For individuals with a condition that requires *severe fat restriction*, avocados may need to be avoided temporarily.
- **Dried Fruits** (Added oil- and sugar-free varieties): Eat moderately.

b. Nuts and Seeds such as:

Coconut, macadamia: Use sparingly to avoid excess calorie consumption.

c. Gluten:

For the 1% to 2% of the population with celiac disease, a gluten-free diet rich in fruits and vegetables, legumes and dried beans, plant protein sources, nuts, seeds, and nondairy alternatives rich in calcium and vitamin D, plays an important role in management of symptoms, and to reduce morbidity and mortality.[146]

d. Coffee:

Maximum of 1 cup of coffee (two cups of decaf, or one ounce of espresso) daily. Inclusion of a limited amount of caffeine also includes the option for up to two cups of tea.[147] (see *Water and Other Beverages > Tea*).

A whole food, plant-based nutrition pattern eliminates many factors that deplete energy such as simple and refined carbohydrates, processed foods, high-fat foods, and meat and dairy; therefore, the need for a daily energy boost is unnecessary.

Note:

- Coffee-based drinks may be loaded with added sugars and fats that reduce their health benefits and should be avoided.
- Caffeine should be avoided if you're sensitive to caffeine, have a history of high blood pressure, anxiety, or arrhythmias, insomnia, gastro-esophageal reflux, if you're taking certain medications, and if indicated by your physician. It is important to discuss caffeine intake with your physician.[148]
- Energy drinks containing caffeine should be avoided. (see *Processed Beverages*)

e. Plant-based Foods such as:

Seitan (wheat gluten protein), due to gluten intolerance should be avoided.

F. FOODS TO AVOID

a. Animal-derived foods:

- **Meats:** [149] [150] [151] [152] [153] [154] [155]
  Fish, poultry, seafood, beef, pork, lamb, processed meat, etc.

- **Dairy:** [156] [157]
  Yogurt, milk, cheese, half and half, cream, buttermilk, butter, mayonnaise.

- **Eggs:** [158] [159] [160] [161]
  Hen, quail, or other animal eggs.

Notes:

A significant number of studies including the NHS (Nurses' Health Study) and HPFS (Health Professionals Follow-up Study) suggest a substantial increased risk of mortality with higher trans and saturated fat intakes with all sources of animal protein (eggs, fish, poultry, red meat, and processed red meat). These were noted to increase all-cause mortality relative to vegetable protein, with processed red meat being associated with more cardiovascular deaths and egg consumption being associated with more cancer deaths.[162]

b. Processed Foods:

A "processed food" is the result of one or various elements that have been extracted from their original source such as soy protein isolate. (see *Whole-ism vs. Reductionism*)

- **Added fats:**
  Solid and liquid oils such as canola, olive, palm,[163] avocado, almond, or coconut oil[164] and other fats such as margarine, butter, lard.

- **Processed Food Products**
  - Highly processed foods with significant amounts of added fat, sugar and salt
  - Refined grain products (e.g., white flour and white rice products)
  - Fried foods

- **Refined flours:**
  Any flours that are not 100% whole

- **Refined sugars and foods:**
  - Candy bars, many types of snack/energy bars, cookies, cakes, pastries
  - White sugar and other processed sweeteners

- **Processed Beverages:**
  - Sugary drinks, soda, processed fruit juices, sports drinks
  - Sugar-based drinks with coffee and tea ingredients
  - Energy drinks (mixtures of vitamins and caffeine or caffeine-containing compounds), increase the risk of adverse health effects ranging from arrhythmia, coronary spasm, and even death,[165] and have been associated with increased morbidity and mortality, especially in young individuals.[166] All energy drinks greatly surpass (by 2 to 4 times) the U.S. Food and Drug Administration (FDA) approved concentration of caffeine permissible in a soft drink.[167]

c. Alcoholic Beverages (Wine, liquor, beer):

Alcohol consumption should be avoided completely for individuals with any type of health condition. Healthy individuals should avoid alcohol or limit consumption to one or two servings (<1 ounce) per week. Among women, there are limited data suggesting that even modest alcohol consumption is associated with increased risk of developing breast cancer.[168]

G. MEAL PLANNING

A common concern when considering any nutritional pattern, including an entirely plant-based one, is nutrient adequacy. The Academy of Nutrition and Dietetics states in their position paper:[169] "Vegetarian diets, including vegan diets, are healthful, nutritionally adequate, and may provide health benefits for the prevention and treatment of certain diseases. These diets are appropriate for all stages of the life cycle, including pregnancy, lactation, infancy, childhood, adolescence, older adulthood, and for athletes." Even calorie-restricted plant-based diets intended for weight loss, have been found to be consistent with dietary guidelines.[170]

A low fat, whole food, plant-based dietary habit does not concern itself with singular nutrients such as the quantity of protein, calcium, or other nutrients because all available nutrients to sustain life are available in plant foods.[171] Therefore, consuming a variety of whole foods will provide all the nutritional needs for humans and ensure a plethora of antioxidants and macronutrients for health and wellbeing.

It is crucial to recognize that all plants, and in this case, whole foods (vegetables, legumes, whole grains, fruits, nuts, seeds) contain all three macronutrients, namely, carbohydrates, protein, and fat. It is a pervasive misunderstanding to identify a food as a "carb," "protein," or "fat." Instead, these are all nutrients within a complex of other myriad constituents that are beyond the reductionism promoted by our system.[172] [173] (see *Whole-ism vs. Reductionism*)

Protein seems to be a frequent target for informational inadequacy; therefore, it is fundamental to emphasize that all plants contain protein in variable amounts. Pound for pound (dry weight), vegetable protein-rich foods, such as legumes, contain as much or more protein than most animal foods, without the sodium or fat.[174] One cup of cooked lentils contains 18g of protein (and no fat or sodium). For comparison, an average 6-oz steak may have up to 40g protein, but also has 12g of saturated fatty acids (SFAs), which is nearly two-thirds of the recommended daily allotment.[175]

It is not necessary to intentionally combine or "complement" plant foods to obtain adequate protein.[176] Although the quantities of essential amino acids vary from one food to another, nearly all plant-derived foods contain the 9 essential amino acids needed for human health.

Including foods from a variety of plant sources can provide adequate quantities of all necessary nutrients with simple diet planning.

H. SUBSTITUTIONS FOR COMMON FOODS

Milk Substitutes.

Opt for non-dairy milks such as rice, oat, hemp, nut, and grain milks. Coconut milk is also acceptable, but because of its fat content it should be used sparingly.

Sugar Substitutes.

Use fresh fruit as natural sweetener, or dried fruit (oil- and sugar-free varieties) such as dates, figs, cranberries, apricots, prunes, and raisins.

Oil Substitutes.

- Baking without Oil: Replace the oil in a recipe with half the amount of another moist food, such as apple sauce, mashed bananas, mashed potatoes, mashed pumpkin, or tomato sauce.
- Sautéing without Oil: Replace the oil with vegetable broth, water, apple cider, sherry, rice vinegar, white or red wine, or lemon juice.

Pasta Substitutes

Use whole grain, quinoa, buckwheat, rice, and plant-based varieties, and choose gluten-free in case of gluten intolerance. Whole fresh foods such as sweet potatoes, carrots, zucchini, and squash also make great raw or cooked pasta substitutes.

Egg Substitutes

- Baking without eggs:
  - 1 egg equals ½ banana, or ¼ pureed fruit
  - 1 egg equals 1 tablespoon ground flax seed + 3 tablespoons water
  - 1 egg equals 1 teaspoon ground chia seeds + 3 tablespoons water

- Cooking without eggs:
  - For quiche, non-egg scrambles, and frittatas, use organic, non-GMO tofu.

Meat Substitutes

Tofu, Seitan, and Tempeh.

Both tofu and tempeh are based on soybeans; therefore, if used, they should come from organic, and non-GMO sources. These are both high in protein, omega-3s, iron, and fiber and are gluten-free. Seitan is made of wheat protein, or gluten, not recommended in case of gluten intolerance.

Cheese Substitutes

Nuts and seeds make great cheese alternatives. Sunflower and pumpkin seeds as well as cashews, pine nuts, chestnuts, or almonds blended with onion, garlic, miso, tamari, herbs, legumes, and cooked potatoes can satisfy any cheese craving. Nutritional Yeast is cultured yeast from molasses and sugar cane. It is also a good source of B12 and protein and can be used as a cheese-flavoring ingredient.

CASHEW CREAM CHEESE

(Recipe by Naked Food Magazine)

Yield: 1/2 cup

Ingredients

- 2/3 cup raw cashews, soaked overnight or quick-soaked in hot water for 10 minutes
- 2 peeled garlic cloves
- 1 tablespoon fresh lemon juice
- 1 to 2 teaspoons dried rosemary (or your favorite herb), optional
- 3 teaspoons nutritional yeast
- Water, as needed

Method

Combine all ingredients in a high-power blender or food processor. Add water in 1-tablespoon increments as needed to achieve the desired consistency. This cheese recipe turns out as a great cream cheese dip or spread and can be used in pasta recipes such as Cacio e Pepe or Alfredo sauce.

Salt Substitutes

Low-sodium, non-GMO miso paste and rice miso, salt-free seasoning, shoyu, and tamari, are good salt alternatives for a wide variety of recipes.

I. MEAL EXAMPLES

The emphasis of a wholistic, well-planned, and healthful meal must be on the quality of the totality of foods coming from whole plant sources as opposed to calculations and perfect ratios[177] and should, therefore, include sufficient vegetables, fruits, legumes, grains, and some nuts or seeds to enhance absorption of nutrients.[178]

STUFFED SWEET POTATO

1 sweet potato topped with garbanzo beans, chili salsa or tomato filling, avocado, fresh parsley or cilantro and a large green salad sprinkled with nuts and seeds.

VEGGIE WRAP

1-4 sprouted or whole wheat veggie wraps with hummus or beans, avocado and sweet potato, raw vegetables, fresh sprouts and seeds.

OATMEAL BOWL

1/2 cup of rolled oats with fresh or frozen berries, a few nuts, and plant-based milk blended with cacao, banana, and 1 Tbsp. ground chia or flax seeds.

TOFU SCRAMBLE

1 tofu scramble on toasted sprouted or whole wheat bread with guacamole and vegetables as desired and a side green salad.

GREEN VEGETABLE SMOOTHIE

1 vegetable-based smoothie with kale, broccoli, spinach or swiss chard, 1-2 fruits of your choice, and 1 Tbsp. flax meal (freshly crushed flax seeds).

STUFFED PUMPKIN

2 cups of baked or steamed pumpkin with whole grains such as quinoa or brown rice, mushrooms, vegetables, nuts and seeds of your choice.

GRAIN AND LEGUME BOWL

1 cup cooked grains (such as buckwheat, quinoa, black rice), 1 cup legumes of your choice, sprouts and vegetables as desired with oil-free tahini dressing.

KALE AND LEGUME SALAD

1 large salad with greens and colorful vegetables, sprouts, steamed cubed yams or whole grains (e.g., quinoa or kamut berries), lentil beans or tofu, and hummus for dressing.

VEGGIE BURGER

1 grilled or baked vegetable patty made with raw and cooked vegetables, topped with hummus or avocado, tomato, onion, leafy greens of your choice and sprouted grain bread.

HEARTY VEGETABLE SOUP

2-3 cups of cooked or raw vegetables with legumes such as lentils, beans or chickpeas, leafy greens such as spinach or swiss chard, with vegetables and spices of your choice.

WHOLE GRAIN PASTA

2 cups of whole grain pasta with oil-free vegetable pesto (such as arugula, spinach, or dock) fresh tomato and herbs.

STUFFED MUSHROOMS

1-3 grilled or baked portobello mushrooms stuffed with a whole grain such as quinoa or rice, tomato-based sauce, vegetables of your choice and whole grain breadcrumbs as topping.

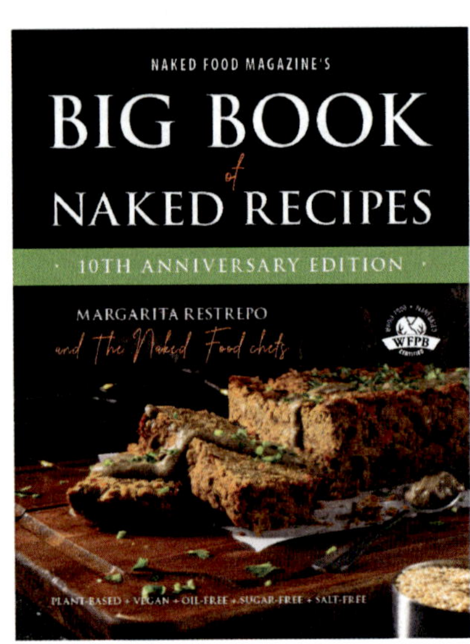

Note!

The Big Book of Naked Recipes

For further meal examples, recipes, tips and advice please check out the Universal Guideline for Human Health companion cookbook: **The Big Book of Naked Recipes**. It features over 400 pages and more than 200 recipes for healthful and delicious food with the potential to prevent and also reverse health conditions. One of the most anticipated cookbooks of its kind, the Big Book of Naked Recipes is a mouth-watering compilation of flavors and tastes for every chef in the family, from beginner to advanced. Scan the QR Code or visit nakedfoodmagazine.com to get your copy.

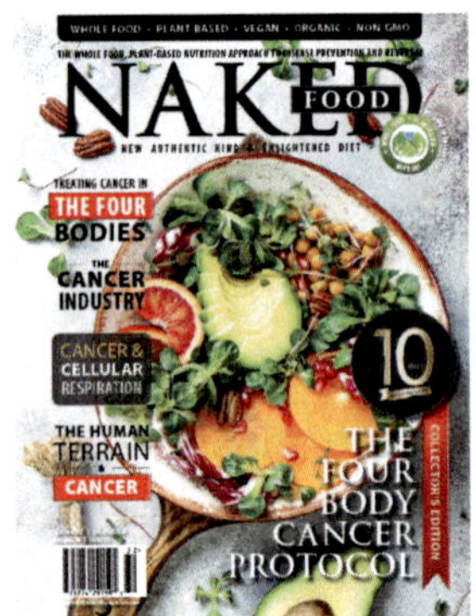

Naked Food Magazine

Another recommended source for recipes and advice is Naked Food Magazine. Please visit Naked Food Magazine's website at www.nakedfoodmagazine.com and subscribe to the publication in digital or printed edition. It features a great variety of whole food, plant-based recipes, tips and ideas for whole meals that aim to maintain optimum health as well as to prevent and reverse any health conditions through lifestyle changes. Naked Food is an independent, nonpartisan, nonreligious, and non-biased publication that reports evidence-based content pertaining to human and planetary health. It performs independent journalistic research on the variety of subjects that it reports, and it does not base its statements in mainstream sources.

Other Recommended Whole Food, Plant-based Cookbooks

Please also browse through the variety of cookbooks (available at nakedfoodmagazine.com) in digital and print formats such as **The Wholiday Cookbook, The Wholeoween Cookbook, The Master Plants Cookbook,** and **The Naked Food Cookbook.**

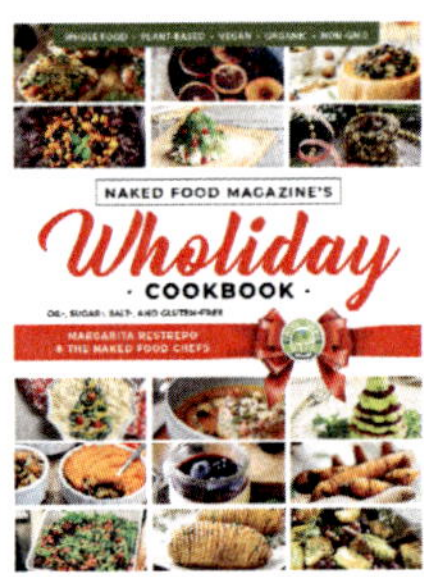

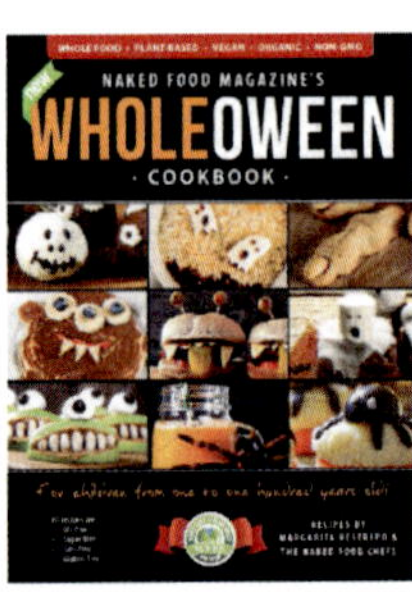

OTHER HEALTH RECOMMENDATIONS

Fasting

Fasting is primarily a rest of the organism.[179] Rest gives all the organs an opportunity to repair the damaged structures, and there is no condition of disease in which rest of vital organs is not a benefit to the whole organism. Fasting means a temporary cessation of the inflow of nutritive substances. This gives the surfeited organism an opportunity to consume its surplus which results in increased vigor and improved function.[180] [181] Also called *Denutrition*, temporary abstinence from food is the most effective, and at the same time, the safest method for eliminating morbid elements from the system.

Fasting has been a natural practice throughout animal and human evolution, and it is often used for religious or spiritual reasons, including in Islam, Christianity, Judaism and Buddhism.[182] Animals in hibernation go through long periods of food restriction. Humans evolved to be able to function when food was not available for extended periods of time.

What Fasting Does

Fasting is usually understood as the ingestion of water only. It is a therapy that enables the organism to stop all mechanisms that may be causing a problem by allowing it to rebalance and heal itself.[183] [184] What and how does fasting do that?

- It gives the vital organs a complete rest.
- It stops the intake of foods that decompose in the intestines and further poison the body.
- It empties the digestive track and disposes of putrefactive bacteria.
- It gives the organs of elimination time to catch up with their work and promotes elimination and detoxification
- It reestablishes normal physiological chemistry and secretions
- It promotes the breaking down and absorption of exudate effusion deposits and diseased tissues in abnormal growth
- It restores a useful condition and function of the cells and tissues
- It rejuvenates the body
- It permits the conservation and recanalization of energy
- It increases the powers of digestion and assimilation
- It clears and strengthens the mind
- It improves function throughout the body

Fasting consists of **correcting the lifestyle errors that have brought on and perpetuated the toxemia in the body**. These errors are not all errors in eating alone. Worry, excesses, dissipations, etc., have as much to do with producing sickness as wrong eating.[185] Because of this, it is important to address mental and emotional health and create self-reliant tools that induce stress relief, peace and relaxation, meditation, and positive environments around us.

Scientifically, the evidence suggests that a water-only fasting, results in a variety of beneficial health promoting physiological effects[186] including detoxification, ketogenesis, hormone modulation, reduced oxidative stress and inflammation, and increased stress resistance, lipolysis, and autophagy.[187] [188] [189] [190] Water fasting has also shown significant improvement in conditions such as hypertension,[191] [192] rheumatoid arthritis,[193] cardiovascular disease,[194] [195] metabolic syndrome,[196] [197] osteoarthritis,[198] fibromyalgia,[199] chronic pain,[200] and overall quality of life.[201]

A study from Intermountain Medical Center showed that people who partook in a 24-hour fast had between a 1,300% to 2,000% increase in Human Growth Hormone (HGH).[202] HGH, produced by the pituitary gland, spurs growth in children and adolescents. It also helps to regulate body composition, body fluids, muscle and bone growth, sugar and fat metabolism, and possibly heart function. HGH works to protect lean muscle and metabolic balance, a response triggered and accelerated by fasting.

Water-only fasting and an exclusively plant-food diet has been beneficial in the management of stage IIIa, low-grade follicular lymphoma[203] and the cessation of many other types of cancer. Water fasting stimulates biological mechanisms in humans that may potentiate tumor regression, such as decreasing levels of leptin and insulin-like growth factor 1 (IGF-1).[204] [205]

Intermittent Fasting

Intermittent fasting is an eating pattern that cycles between periods of fasting and eating. It focuses on *when* eating should be done and has powerful effects on the body and brain; it increases longevity[206] [207] [208] while reducing the risk of type 2 diabetes, heart disease, and cancer. Intermittent fasting may not only prevent cancer[209] [210] [211] [212] but studies suggest that it is safe and capable of decreasing toxicity and tumor growth.[213]

Common intermittent fasting methods involve daily 16-hour fasts or fasting for 24 hours, once or twice per week. During the fasting periods, you eat either very little or ideally, nothing at all. The most popular methods include:

- **The 16/8 method:** Also called the *Leangains Protocol*, it involves skipping breakfast and restricting your daily eating period to 8 hours, such as 11-7 p.m. or 1–9 p.m. Then you fast for 16 hours in between.
- **Eat-Stop-Eat:** This involves fasting for 24 hours once or twice a week, for example by not eating from dinner one day until dinner the next day.
- **The 5:2 diet:** With this method, you consume only 500–600 calories on two nonconsecutive days of the week and eat normally the other 5 days.

It is recommended to do water-only fasting and intermittent fasting as often as needed. For more information and counseling on how to fast please see the Coaching Section on this guideline.

Sunshine (Vitamin D)

Essential production of Vitamin D within the human body occurs with natural sun exposure during the summer months. The Minimal Erythemicdose Dose (MED) is the level of exposure to sun that causes the skin to become slightly pink, after which 10,000-20,000 IU vitamin D is released into circulation within 24 hours. For people who live in northern latitudes, vitamin D requirements in winter are met with stored vitamin D from exposure in the summer.

Vitamin D is a main prerequisite to the absorption of calcium and phosphorus from the intestines and is therefore important in the remineralization of the bones. It helps to regulate blood clotting, optimizes the function of the nerves and muscles, and affects the skin, pancreas, glandular function, and immune system.

In humans, vitamin D3 synthesized in the epidermis and is taken up into the bloodstream tightly bound to a vitamin D-binding protein. Both vitamin D3 (derived from sun exposure and dietary sources) and vitamin D2 (derived only from dietary sources) are metabolized in the liver.

Cholesterol-free sources of vitamin D include chanterelle mushrooms, shiitake mushrooms, plant-based supplements, and fortified whole grain cereals and plant milks.[214]

The Institute of Medicine (US) Committee recommends an average of 4,000 IU (100 μg) daily Dietary intake for Vitamin D,[215] but our recommendation varies depending on season and/or geographical location.

Northern Latitudes:[216]

Vitamin D supplementation for those living in Northern latitudes **who cannot** make vitamin D from sunshine for several months of the year.

a. Below approximately **30°** latitude (south of Los Angeles / Atlanta / Cairo / Delhi / Shanghai). Includes latitudes of Mexico City / Bogotá / Lagos / Bangkok / Hong Kong / Manila.

- 15-30 minutes of midday sun (15 for those with lighter skin; 30 for those with darker skin) or 2,000 IU supplemental vitamin D daily

b. Between **30°** latitude (sample cities above) and **40°** latitude (Portland /Chicago /Boston /Rome /Beijing)

- From February through November, 15-30 minutes of midday sun (15 for those with lighter skin; 30 for those with darker skin) or 2,000 IU supplemental vitamin D daily
- From December through January, 2,000 IU supplemental vitamin D daily

c. Between **40°** latitude (Portland / Montreal / Rome / Beijing) and **50°**latitude (Edmonton / London / Berlin / Moscow)

- From March through October, 15-30 minutes of midday sun (15 for those with lighter skin; 30 for those with darker skin), or 2,000 IU supplemental vitamin D daily
- From November through February, 2,000 IU supplemental vitamin D daily

d. Above approximately **50°** latitude (north of Edmonton/London/Berlin/Moscow)

- From April through September above **60°** latitude (Anchorage/Stockholm/St. Petersburg), 15-30 minutes of midday sun (15 for those with lighter skin; 30 for those with darker skin) or 2,000 IU supplemental vitamin D daily
- From October through March above **60°** latitude (Anchorage/Stockholm/St. Petersburg), 2,000 IU supplemental vitamin D daily

Notes:

- There is not enough evidence to support a recommendation for food fortification or widespread vitamin D supplementation for the general population. Unlike vitamin D produced in the skin, there is the potential that vitamin D from supplements and fortificants could build up to toxic levels and there is not enough evidence about the possible risks of raised vitamin D blood levels in the general population over a long period of time.
- Vitamin D produced by skin remains in circulation 2-3 times longer than when taken as a supplement. Taken in supplement form 100 IU of vitamin D only increases plasma levels less than 1 ng/mL.
- An average of 30-70 ng/mL is optimal for bone health, tissue health, and immune health among others.

Vitamin B12

Cobalamin, commonly referred to as vitamin B12, is the only nutrient not directly available from plants. This is because vitamin B12 is synthesized by microorganisms, bacteria, fungi, and algae, but not by plants or animals. Animals consume these microorganisms along with their food, which is why this vitamin can be found in their meat, organs, and by-products (eggs and dairy).[217]

Fermented foods, spirulina, chlorella, certain mushrooms, and sea vegetables, among other foods, can provide some B12, but in most cases, one of the most reliable method of avoiding deficiency is to take a B12 supplement. Because the body can absorb only approximately 1.5 µg to 2.0 µg at a time, it is ideal to supplement with a dose greater than the Recommended Dietary Allowance (RDA) to ensure adequate intake. Experts recommend a total weekly dose of 2,000 µg to 2,500 µg. This can be split into daily doses or into 2 to 3 doses of 1000 µg each per week to help enhance absorption. Because vitamin B12 is water soluble, toxicity is rare.

The general recommendation is 2,500mcg vitamin supplement weekly or 250 mcg (2.4 µg) daily to ensure sufficient absorption.[218] Higher doses of Vitamin B12 may be necessary in those who are deficient or have a malabsorption disorder. Researchers suggest the assessment of methylmalonic acid and homocysteine during the evaluation of patients with suspected deficiencies of vitamin B12 and folate.[219] Vitamin B12 is essential for many functions including the formation of amino acids, neurotransmitters, and erythrocytes.

The Recommended Daily Allowance of B12 should be in the form of methylcobalamin (not cyanocobalamin) and includes:[220]

For children:

- 1–3 years 0.9 µg/day
- 4–8 years 1.2 µg/day

RDA for Boys

- 9–13 years 1.8 µg/day
- 14–18 years 2.4 µg/day

RDA for Girls

- 9–13 years 1.8 µg/day
- 14–18 years 2.4 µg/day

For pregnant women:

- **Daily:** 2.6 (µg) daily of supplemental methylcobalamin

For adults up to 50 years old:

- **Weekly:** 2,500 mcg (μg) methylcobalamin once each week, ideally as a chewable, sublingual, or liquid supplement taken on an empty stomach ***or,***
  Daily: 2.4 (μg) daily of supplemental methylcobalamin ***or,***
- Servings of B12-fortified foods three times a day, each containing at least 25% U.S. "Daily Value" on its label.

For adults over 51 years old:

- 1,000 mcg (μg) methylcobalamin every day.
- The EAR[221] and RDA[222] for B12 for adults ages 51 years and older are the same as for younger adults but with the recommendation that B12-fortified foods (such as fortified ready-to-eat cereals) or B12-containing supplements be used to meet much of the requirement.

Notes:

If experiencing deficiency symptoms of Vitamin B12, the best test is a urine methylmalonic acid (**MMA**) test (not serum B12 level).

Omega-3 Fatty Acids

Essential fatty acids are found in various plants. The aim is a daily consumption of omega-3-rich plant foods such as seeds like flax seed (see *Seeds*), soybeans and soybean products such as tofu (see *Legumes*), seaweed (see *Seaweed*), and/or nuts (see *Nuts*).

Calcium

At least 1,000 mg daily for adults, age 19 to 50 years old, via calcium-rich plant foods. Women older than 50 and men aged 70 and beyond, should increase their daily intake to 1,200 milligrams. Exercise and daily activity contribute to calcium absorption and protect the bones.[223] (see *Physical Activity*)

Calcium rich foods include:

- Tofu, 350mg per ½ cup serving
- Tapioca, 300mg per ½ cup serving
- Chia seeds, 300mg per 1.5 ounces serving
- Collard greens, 210mg per ½ cup serving
- Kale, 205mg per ½ cup serving
- Bok Choy, 190mg per ½ cup serving
- Figs, 135mg per 5-fig serving
- White Beans, 120mg per ½ cup serving
- Turnip Greens, 104mg per ½ cup serving
- Spinach, 99mg per ½ cup serving
- Almonds, 93mg per ¼ cup serving
- Sesame, 88mg per tablespoon serving
- Sweet Potatoes, 76mg per cup serving
- Broccoli, 42mg per cup serving

Protein

Though protein provides the raw material for many of the functional and structural components of the body, a human does not need to ingest the muscle of another animal in order to build its own muscle, as all dietary proteins —including those from plants— are enzymatically broken apart to individual amino acids, and then reconstructed into the precise protein structures human tissues may require.

Plants, not animals, are the original sources of all amino acids.

There are 22 amino acids currently identified as necessary for the health of the human body. The nine essential amino acids (necessary to acquire through diet), and twelve nonessential amino acids (synthesized within the body) are all found in sufficient amounts in a variety of plant foods.

Protein is readily available throughout the plant kingdom, but those foods that are particularly rich in protein include legumes, nuts and nut butters, seeds and seed butters, soy foods, and intact whole grains.

Iodine

Adequate dietary iodine is required for normal thyroid function, to keep a strong immune system, and to promote wound healing. The recommended daily allowance through the consumption of sea vegetables like wakame, kelp, arame, or dulse[224] is as follows.[225]

Recommendation for iodine:

- Infants aged 7–11 months: 130 μg/day
- School children and adults 150 μg/day
- Pregnant and lactating women 200 μg/day

Notes:

- One half teaspoon of iodized salt provides the daily recommended 150 μg dose[226] (see *Added Sodium*)
- The best test for iodine deficiency is a 24-hour urine collection. Deficiency is considered to be less than 100 mcg excreted in 24 hours.
- Goitrogens are substances that interfere with iodine utilization or thyroid hormone production. Cruciferous vegetables (cabbage, broccoli, cauliflower, and Brussels sprouts), soybeans, pine nuts, millet, and leafy greens contain goitrogens. Steaming, cooking, or fermenting these foods reduces the levels of goitrogens in goitrogenic foods. With adequate iodine intake, goitrogens pose no problem to the thyroid of healthy individuals. Furthermore, research indicates that a substance found in cruciferous vegetables, 3,3'-Diidolylmethane (DIM), has anti-proliferative effects in glandular thyroid proliferative disease.[227]
- If an individual does not enjoy sea vegetables or is minimizing intake of salt, an iodine supplement may be warranted.[228]

Iron

There is a wide array of iron-rich food choices in the plant kingdom. Leafy greens, beets, beet greens, and legumes are excellent sources of iron and myriad other nutrients. Other good choices include soy-based products, dark chocolate, blackstrap molasses, tahini, pumpkin seeds, sunflower seeds, raisins, prunes, and cashews.

Notes:

- In order to enhance absorption, consume iron-rich foods in combination with foods high in vitamin C and organic acid-rich foods. This combination improves solubility, thereby facilitating absorption.
- All menstruating women should increase their absorption by combining foods rich in iron and vitamin C at meals, such as squeezing lemon juice over steamed broccoli or adding mandarin orange slices to a spinach salad.
- Women should have a blood test for iron-deficiency anemia every few years, or whenever symptoms might be present (weakness, pallor, low energy)
- Men should be checked for an iron overload disease (serum iron, ferritin, hemoglobin, etc.) before any attempt to increase iron intake.
- Supplementation without documented deficiency is not recommended on any population group.

Selenium

Northern Europeans may need to take a supplement or eat a daily Brazil nut.[229] A single Brazil nut can provide more than twice the Recommended Dietary Allowance (RDA) of selenium. A large nut has 140 micrograms, or 254 percent of the RDA.

2. PHYSICAL ACTIVITY

Physical activity is defined as any bodily movement produced by skeletal muscles that results in energy expenditure. More specifically, exercise is a subset of physical activity that is planned, structured, and repetitive and has as a final or an intermediate objective: the improvement or maintenance of physical fitness. Physical fitness is a set of attributes that are either health or skill related.

Exercising has been shown to have several advantages for human health and well-being. Several studies have highlighted its benefits, the main ones include:

- **Reduction of Muscle Loss.** Exercise increases muscle, tendon and ligament strength. As people age, they tend to lose muscle mass, strength, and function, which leads to an increased risk of injury. Practicing regular physical activity and exercise is essential to reducing muscle loss and maintaining strength as you age.
- **Increase in Bone Density.** Exercise also helps build bone density. The authors of a recent review found that regular exercise significantly improved bone density in the lumbar spine, neck, and hip bones. This may help prevent osteoporosis later in life.
- **Increase in Energy Levels.** The heart pumps more blood as the body moves, delivering more oxygen to the working muscles. With regular exercise, the heart becomes more efficient at moving oxygen into the blood.
- **Increase in Happiness.** Exercise has been shown to improve mood and decrease feelings of depression, anxiety, and stress.
- **Help with weight management.** Inactivity plays a major role in weight gain and obesity, which leads to health complications. Exercise can help manage weight by helping to increase energy expenditure and metabolic rate.
- **Lower Risk of Disease.** Exercise reduces the risk of chronic diseases, like diabetes, cancer and hypertension.
- **Improvement of Brain Function.** Vigorous exercise has been shown to promote the secretion of a molecule called BDNF (brain-derived neurotrophic factor). BDNF acts on the neurons of the central nervous system and the peripheral nervous system, helping to support survival of existing neurons, and encouraging growth and differentiation of new neurons and synapses.
- **Enhance Sexual Life.** Physical activity and exercise increase the health of the cardiovascular and circulatory system. It also stimulates the production of nitric oxide, which is a key factor for a good sexual life. Exercising will benefit both you and your loved one. ;)

From a physical standpoint, to live a quality and enjoyable life we need our body to be able to easily handle any type of stress or challenge that day-to-day life requires. For example, daily activities may include working in a factory, playing with the grandchildren, fixing the garden, swimming in the ocean, carrying the groceries, riding a bike or going for a hike. In all those cases our body needs to be healthy and strong to accomplish the task easily and without too much effort. Keeping the body healthy and strong for as long as possible means being able to be self-sufficient and enjoy life for as long as possible. This is a key factor in determining the quality of life of any individual.

Ideally, the body, and more specifically its physical capacity, should never be what limits an individual or goes against him/her. Instead, the body should be the vehicle through which you can experience life and pursue happiness.

General Recommendation

The general recommendation is to perform 45-60 minutes of exercise 5-6 days per week, making sure to include all the following training modalities:

- Flexibility and Mobility Training
- Strength-oriented Resistance Training
- Low to Moderate Intensity Aerobic Training

Each one of these exercise categories aims to improve a specific physical quality. All three of the exercise categories should be executed regularly to ensure the best physical state possible needed to live a pleasant and happy life.

a. Flexibility and Mobility Training

The term *flexibility* generally refers to muscles and their capacity to lengthen, while the term *mobility* usually refers to the joint and its ability to move. However, since the two concepts are strongly linked to one another, the terms mobility and flexibility are often used interchangeably.

Mobility/flexibility training has the potential to increase the length a muscle can reach and therefore it allows a given joint to move through a larger range of motion (also called ROM). This ability is key for every kind of activity. Developing greater mobility and flexibility through proper and specific training means being able to move better in every plane of movement.

Mobility/flexibility training has a very low impact on the body if done properly, and therefore, it can be done almost every day and requires little to no equipment.

Mobility and Flexibility Exercises

There are hundreds of mobility and flexibility exercises commonly used in fitness-related environments like gyms, yoga classes, dancing classes etc. However, performing just a few of them while making sure to cover every main area of the body is enough to achieve better movement capacity.
Listed below you find the main recommended exercises:

1. Kneeling Spine Mobilization
2. Quad and Psoas Stretch
3. Adductors Stretch
4. Hamstrings and Posterior Chain Stretch
5. Lats and Thoracic Spine Stretch

1. Kneeling Spine Mobilization

Recommendation: Perform 2 Sets of 12 repetitions each, resting 30 seconds in between sets.

Image 1

Image 2

How to Execute the Exercise:

Place yourself on the floor in a kneeling position. Make sure to have the wrists directly under the shoulders, and the knees directly under the hips. To start the exercise, extend the spine while looking up as shown in image 1. Then, flex the spine while looking down as shown in image 2. This exercise must be performed slowly.

2. Quad and Psoas Stretch

Recommendation: Perform 2 Sets of 30 seconds hold for each leg, resting 15 seconds in between sets.

Image 3

How to Execute the Exercise:

Place one foot in front with the leg bent at 90 degrees. Place the other foot against a wall as shown in image 3, making sure the back knee is close to the wall. Bring the hips as close as possible to the back foot and hold the position for 30 seconds. Repeat the exercise on the other leg.

3. Adductors Stretch

Recommendation: Perform 3 Sets of 30 seconds hold, resting 30 seconds in between sets

Image 4

Image 5

How to Execute the Exercise:

Place the elbows and knees on the floor as shown in image 4. Both legs are bent at 90 degrees with the toes pointing out to the side as shown on image 5. Spread the knees outward as much as possible while bringing the hips toward the floor. Make sure to align hips and knees while holding the position without bringing the hips forward.

4. Hamstrings and Posterior Chain Stretch

Recommendation: Perform 3 Sets of 30 seconds hold, resting 30 seconds in between sets.

Image 6

How to Execute the Exercise:

Sit on the floor with the feet against the wall and the legs completely straight. Reach forward with your hands aiming to touch the feet as shown in image 6. Don't worry if you are not able to reach the feet. Simply lean forward as far as you can. With time, you will get there. If you are able to reach the feet easily, try progressing by bringing your face toward the shins.

5. Lats and Thoracic Spine Stretch

Recommendation: Perform 3 Sets of 30 seconds hold, resting 30 seconds in between sets.

Image 7

How to Execute the Exercise:

Place your hands on a support with a height similar to that of your hips. Position your feet far from the support as shown in Image 7. Push your head down and drop the chest toward the floor. While doing this, push yourself away from the support. This will put the shoulders in a better and safer position.

Note! You can perform all these exercises every day of the week. The higher the frequency, the more benefits they will bring. While you stretch you should just feel normal muscle tension caused by the position, however, make sure you don't feel any pain or discomfort to prevent injury.

b. Strength-oriented Resistance Training

Strength is the capacity of one or more muscles to produce force in a specific direction. Producing force in a specific direction is what allows us to walk, run, lift a bag or get up from a chair. It is understood from this definition, that strength is a fundamental physical quality for everyday life, and we need a certain degree or strength to complete each and every physical task.

Resistance training is the type of training that uses either an external or internal load (such as using bodyweight against gravity) to stimulate one or more muscles in the body to make them stronger. However, muscles are not the only tissue that is targeted by resistance training.

Although they may not be visible to the naked eye, there are many structures and tissues of the body that benefit from this type of exercise. Bones become stronger as well when a load is placed upon the body. The matrix of which the skeleton is made of can become denser if the right exercises, with the right intensity, are performed, over time. A strong skeleton is a healthy skeleton. Reaching high bone density through training will drastically decrease the risk of developing bone-related chronic diseases like osteoporosis in the later stages of life.

Connective tissues, like tendons and ligaments, are generally considered strong because they can handle high amounts of force compared to other tissues. Resistance training will provide an adequate amount of stimulus to those tissues, making them grow stronger over time. Having strong ligaments, tendons and cartilages means having healthy joins that can move freely and pain free. This is a key component for longevity.

Increasing Strength

Most people would benefit from increasing their strength levels. Increasing and maintaining strength even in the later stages of life is key to health and self-sufficiency. For example, an individual who performs squats (one of the main lower-body exercises) consistently will be able to add a significant load to the movement over time, let's say 30lb. A squat with 30 added pounds is a goal that pretty much everyone can achieve. If this individual keeps training into his/her 70's, 80's or even further in age, he/she can keep the strength level needed to do a squat with 30lb. Objectively, if one squats that weight, one will for sure be able to go up the stairs on their own and to stand up and walk on their own. This means being able to be self-sufficient even in the late stages of life, which will allow one to live with freedom and joy. This is the most important goal of exercising.

In conclusion, a healthy-looking individual may not be able to squat 30lb. but an individual who can squat 30lb. is undoubtedly healthy. We've collected a list of eleven resistance training exercises plus a sample program that works the whole body. The exercises can be performed at home with minimal equipment and adapted to everyone regardless of one's health and fitness status.

1. Heels Elevated Squats
2. Lunges
3. Reverse Nordics
4. Poliquin Step Ups
5. Nordic Bridges
6. Bodyweight Push Ups
7. Bodyweight Rows
8. Lateral Raises
9. Arched Body
10. Toe Touches
11. Planks

1. Heels Elevated Squats

Recommendation: Perform 4 Sets of 6 to 8 repetitions, resting 2 minutes in between sets.

Image 8 Image 9

Image 10 Image 11

How to Execute the Exercise:

Place the heels on a slight (2 to 3 inch) step and extend the arms to the front (image 8). Flex the legs and descend slowly (like sitting down) while pushing the knees forward (image 9). Go as low as possible trying to sit on the back of the heels. Pause for one to two seconds while remaining down (Image 10). Come back up to the standing position focusing on pushing the shoulders upward (Image 11).

If you struggle to reach the lowest position, simply hold on to one or two supports such as a bench or chair. If the exercise is too easy, hold a dumbbell or weight—as heavy as you need—close to the chest instead of keeping the arms straight forward.

2. Lunges

Recommendation: Perform 3 Sets of 10-12 repetitions for each leg resting 1 minute in between sets.

Image 12

Image 13

Image 14

Image 15

How to Execute the Exercise:

Start by placing one leg in front as shown in images 12 and 14. Descend slowly by bringing the back knee downward to the floor, touching the ground slightly as seen in Images 13 and 15. Go back to the starting position by pushing down to the ground with the front leg. If you struggle with keeping your balance, you can use support such as a tree, table or chair. If the exercise is too easy, hold a dumbbell or weight—as heavy as you need—in each hand.

3. Reverse Nordics

Recommendation: Perform 3 Sets of 6 to 8 repetitions, resting 1 minute in between sets.

Image 16

Image 17

How to Execute the Exercise:

Go downward with your knees on the floor as shown in image 16. While keeping the body straight, lean backward slowly with the hips and shoulders at the same time. Reach back as far as possible without losing the body line or balance (Image 17). Push down with your feet on the floor to go back to the starting position (Image 16). Lean backwards as much as you can handle. Do not lean too fast or too soon. Take your time to progress with the exercise.

4. Poliquin Step Ups

Recommendation: Perform 3 Sets of 10 to 20 repetitions for each leg resting 1 minute in between sets.

Image 18

Image 19

How to Execute the Exercise:

Find a step (stairs or walkway) of at least 10 inches and stand over the first step. Stand with one leg while keeping the other one straight in the air in front of you as shown in image 18. Reach down to the floor slowly with the front leg touching it slightly but without resting on it (Image 19). Push down with the back foot and go back to the starting position (image 18). Holding on to a support or wall is recommended to prevent balance issues.

5. Nordic Bridge

Recommendation: Perform 3 Sets of 10-30 seconds hold (for each leg, if doing the single leg version of the exercise, shown in Image 22 and 23) resting 1 minute in between sets.

Image 20

Image 21

Image 22

Image 23

How to Execute the Exercise:

Note! This exercise can be performed in two different versions: The double leg version (Image 20 and 21) is easier, and the single leg version is more challenging (image 22-23).

- Double Leg Version: Lay down on the floor with the heels on top of a step as shown in image 20. The step should have 10-15 inches height. By pushing down with the heels, lift the hips off the floor as in image 21.
- Single Leg Version: Lay down on the floor with one heel on top of a step and the other leg slightly lifted as shown in image 22. The step should have 10-15 inches height. By pushing down with the heel, lift the hips off the floor as in image 23.

6. Bodyweight Push Ups

Recommendation: Perform 4 Sets of 6-10 repetitions resting 2 minutes in between sets.

Image 24

Image 25

Image 26

Image 27

How to Execute the Exercise:

Position yourself with the hands spread out at a distance 1.5 times larger than the shoulder width (Image 24 and 26). Make sure to keep the body straight in line as shown in all the images above. Lower the body slowly toward the support touching it with the sternum (image 25 and 27). Push with the hands against the support to lift the body and go to the starting position (image 24 and 26).

Note! The level of difficulty for this exercise can be adjusted by changing the height of the support utilized. The higher the support, the easier the exercise. The lower the support, the harder the exercise. Images 24 and 25 show an easier version with higher support while images 26 and 27 show a harder version with lower support. Choose the height based on your strength and ability after trying various height options.

7. Bodyweight Rows

Recommendation: Perform 4 Sets of 6-10 repetitions resting 2 minutes in between sets.

Image 28

Image 29

Image 30

Image 31

How to Execute the Exercise:

Grab a large towel or a rope and wrap it around a tree, column or light post. Position your feet at the desired distance (see the note below). Keep your body in a straight position while holding on to the towel or rope (image 28 and 30). Pull yourself toward the support used as shown in image 29 and 31. Then slowly go back to the starting position (image 28 and 29).

Note! The difficulty of this exercise can be adjusted by changing the distance to the support utilized. The farther the support, the easier the exercise. The closer the support, the harder the exercise. Images 28 and 29 show an easier version with greater distance from the support while images 30 and 31 show a more difficult version with smaller distance from the support. Choose the distance based on your strength and ability after trying various distance options.

8. Lateral Raises

Recommendation: Perform 3 Sets of 8-12 repetitions resting 1 minutes in between sets.

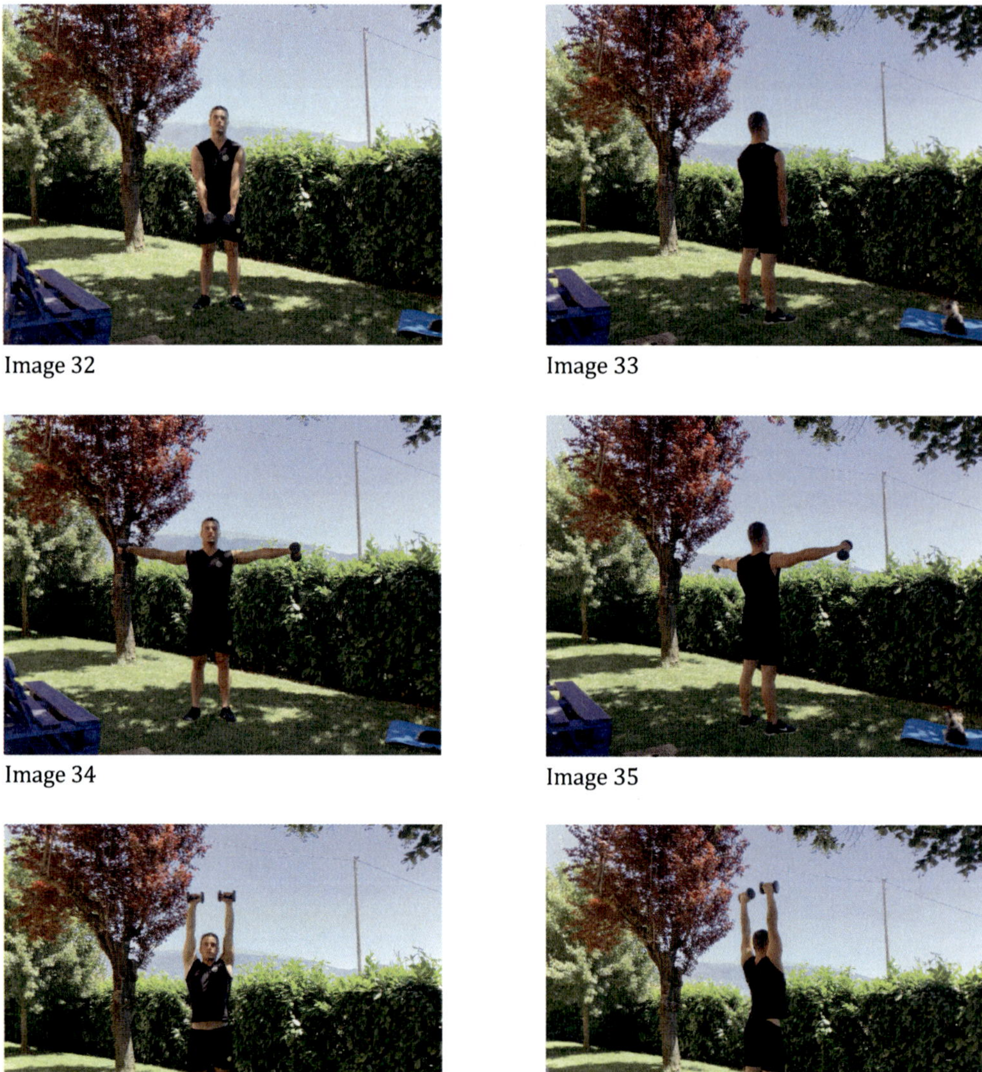

Image 32 Image 33

Image 34 Image 35

Image 36 Image 37

How to Execute the Exercise:

Grab a dumbbell in each hand (as heavy as needed) and put the hands in front of the body with the palms facing each other, as shown in image 32 and 33. With straight arms, start lifting the hands to shoulder level (Image 34 and 35) and then continue the movement lifting them over the head (Image 36 and 37). The movement should look like one fluid motion. After reaching the top position, lower the arms downward slowly to the starting position (Image 32 and 33).

9. Arched Body

Recommendation: Perform 4 sets of 15-30 seconds hold resting 1 minute in between sets.

Image 38

Image 39

How to Execute the Exercise:

Lay on the floor with the arms bent at 90 degrees as shown in image 38. Then, lift the head, arms, shoulders and chest off the floor squeezing the shoulder blades together as shown in image 39.

10. Toe Touches

Recommendation: Perform 4 sets of 10-15 repetitions resting 1 minute in between sets.

Image 40

Image 41

Image 42

Image 43

How to Execute the Exercise:

Lay on the floor as shown in image 40 and 42, based on what feels better for you. Lift your body trying to reach the toes with your hands (image 41 and 43). Whether you touch the toes or not doesn't matter! Then, go back slowly to the starting position (image 40 and 42).

Note! This exercise can be performed in two ways: The easier option is by putting the feet against a wall or tree. The more difficult option is by keeping the legs pointing up straight with no support.

11. Plank

Recommendation: Perform 4 sets of 20-60 seconds hold resting 1 minute in between sets.

Image 44

Image 45

How to Execute the Exercise:

Lay on the floor with your forearms touching the ground and the shoulders bent at 90 degrees, as shown in image 44. Push with the forearms against the ground to lift the hips off the floor, bringing them in line with the whole body (image 45). Make sure to squeeze the abdominal muscles, glutes, and legs while holding the position.

Resistance Training Program Sample:

The following sample consists of a two days per week workout program that includes all the exercises explained before:

DAY 1

1. Flexibility/Mobility work (include all the five exercises explained under the *Flexibility and Mobility Training* section)
2. Heels elevated squats
3. Poliquin step ups
4. Bodyweight push ups
5. Bodyweight rows
6. Lateral raises
7. Plank

DAY 2

1. Flexibility/Mobility work (include all the five exercises explained under the *Flexibility and Mobility Training* section)
2. Lunges
3. Reverse Nordics
4. Nordic bridges
5. Bodyweight rows
6. Bodyweight push ups
7. Arch body
8. Toe touches

Note!

This sample program is just a general recommendation and may not work for everyone. Parameters like exercise selection, training volume and training intensity should be adequately modulated based on the individual's health status and physical characteristics. Ideally, each person should have a customized exercise program specifically built for their needs to guarantee the safety and effectiveness of the training.

WFPB offers individual consultations, assessments and personalized programs that include ongoing guidance and assistance with a trained professional. Please contact PhysicalTraining@wfpb.org for an assessment or further information.

c. Low to Moderate Intensity Aerobic Training

Aerobic training, also known as "cardio training", is a low to medium intensity type of training which consists of cyclical movements (like walking or running) that are repeated for a given amount of time. Cardio training is important to maintain and improve the health of the heart and the cardiovascular system.

The recommended forms of aerobic training are the following:

- Walkıng
- Swimming
- Dancing
- Hiking
- Playing field sports (basketball, volleyball, soccer, baseball etc.)
- Running

Performing cardio training one to three times a week for 30 to 40 minutes is ideal, in one of the forms listed above. The most important factor about choosing which activity one can use as a form of aerobic training is enjoyability. Choose something that you like, so you'll stick to it regularly, week after week.

It is not recommended to perform cardio and resistance training on the same day to avoid adding unnecessary stress to the body. Instead, perform the resistance training program provided in this guideline on Monday and Thursday and the cardio training on Tuesday and Friday, for instance.

3. SLEEP

a. Recommendation for Adults:

Adults 18 years and beyond: 7-9 hours.[230]

b. Recommendation for Children:[231]

- Infants 4 months to 12 months 12 - 16 hours per 24 hours (including naps)
- Children 1 to 2 years: 11 - 14 hours per 24 hours (including naps)
- Children 3 to 5 years: 10 - 13 hours per 24 hours (including naps)
- Children 6 to 12 years: 9 - 12 hours per 24 hours
- Teenagers 13 to 18 years: 8 - 10 hours per 24 hours

c. Sleep Duration and Disease Risk:

Sleep deprivation contributes to several molecular, immune, and neural changes that play a role in disease development. These changes in biological processes in response to chronic sleep deficiency may serve as etiological factors for the development and exacerbation of cardiovascular and metabolic diseases and, ultimately, a shortened lifespan.

Evidence shows that people in developing countries are sleeping on average only 6.8 hours per night, 1.5 fewer hours than a century ago.[232] [233] Recent epidemiological studies have revealed relationships between sleep deprivation and cardiovascular diseases[234] such as hypertension (HT),[235] [236] [237] [238] [239] [240] coronary heart disease (CHD),[241] [242] and diabetes mellitus (DM).[243] [244] [245] [246] [247] [248] [249]

Studies show that mortality rates from ischemic heart disease, cancer, stroke, and all causes combined are lowest for individuals sleeping 7 or 8 hours per night.[250] Sleep deprivation (6 hours or less), or sleep excess (10 hours or more) show a higher death rate.[251]

- Dysregulation of melatonin secretion caused by sleep deprivation is associated with hypertension and impaired glucose tolerance.[252] [253] [254] [255]
- Experimental sleep deprivation causes elevated evening levels of cortisol that may predispose individuals to insulin resistance.[256] [257]
- Sleep disruption has been linked with reduced testosterone levels.[258] Low levels of testosterone have been associated with obesity,[259] elevated levels of insulin and glucose,[260] [261] and Diabetes Mellitus incidence.[262] [263]
- Sleep restriction results in an increase in sympathetic tone, which inhibits pancreatic function.[264] [265]
- Sleep-disordered breathing, a known cause of daytime sleepiness, would be linked to increased sympathetic tone and glucose intolerance.[266]

The quality and duration of sleep relies on how well the pineal gland produces melatonin. This tiny organ regulates daily and seasonal circadian rhythms, the sleep/wake patterns that determine hormone levels, stress levels, and physical performance.

Calcification in the pineal gland is mainly caused by fluoride, which accumulates in the pineal gland more than in any other organ and leads to the formation of phosphate crystals. As a result, less melatonin is produced, and regulation of the wake/sleep cycle gets disturbed.[267]

Furthermore, fluoride hardening accelerates sexual development in children, particularly in girls.[268] A 30-year-old study reported that 40% of American children under 17 were found to have pineal calcification in progress. Since then we've seen children, especially girls, experience the early onset of puberty.[269]

In addition to fluoride, chlorine and bromine also accumulate and damage the pineal gland. Lastly, calcium carbonate, which is usually present in calcium supplements, is one of the main causes of calcification along with fluoride.

d. Habits to improve sleep:

The following are some important habits that can improve sleep health.[270]

- Include plenty of calcium-rich whole foods. The best form of calcium for the human body is in the form of whole foods like sesame seeds, chia seeds, leafy greens like spinach and kale, quinoa, oranges and broccoli to name a few. These are 100% bioavailable, help detoxify the body, and don't cause pineal gland calcification.
- Keep in mind that without enough sunshine (See *Vitamin D*), calcium from supplement sources does not become bioavailable and calcifies human tissue, including the pineal gland.[271]
- Recommendations to eliminating fluoride include using fluoride-free toothpaste, avoiding tap water, and drinking filtered water. A reverse osmosis water filter is a good option for better drinking water quality.
- Be consistent. Go to bed at the same time each night and get up at the same time each morning, including on the weekends.
- Make sure your bedroom is quiet, dark, relaxing, and at a comfortable temperature.
- Remove electronic devices, such as TVs, computers, and smart phones, from the bedroom.
- Avoid large meals, caffeine, and alcohol before bedtime.
- Avoid tobacco/nicotine.
- Exercise. Being physically active during the day can help you fall asleep more easily at night.

4. STRESS MANAGEMENT

Although the understanding that emotions affect physical health dates as far back as the second-century physician Galen and the medieval physician and philosopher Moses Maimonides, modern medicine has largely continued to treat the mind and body as two separate entities.[272] In the past 30 years, however, research into the link between health and emotions, behavior, social and economic status and personality has moved both research and treatment from the fringe of biomedical science into the mainstream. There is no real division between mind and body because of networks of communication that exist between the brain and neurological, endocrine, and immune systems.[273]

Stress reduction techniques such as meditation and breathing as well as body-mind and physical-psychological approaches[274] including relaxation techniques,[275] cognitive or behavioral techniques,[276] mindfulness-based stress reduction,[277] are associated with a decrease of chronic back pain, herniated disks, and sciatica.[278]

A wholistic approach to health is, again, one that includes a physical, emotional, and spiritual approach to healing and reversal of disease.

A. Stretching, Meditation, Deep breathing, Progressive relaxation, and Imagery

These techniques are much more than simple strategies to help cope with or manage stress. They are designed to increase awareness of what is happening inside the individual—physically, emotionally, and spiritually. Increasing awareness extends the human capacity for control over what is happening within. As a result, individuals are better prepared to recognize the symptoms of stress and make changes before developing unhealthy conditions[279] [280] such as heart disease[281] or high blood pressure.[282] Yoga can also be effective in enhancing the functioning of several body systems, including the lower urinary tract.[283] Current data are suggestive of a possible value of meditation and mindfulness techniques for treating symptomatic anxiety,[284] [285] depression,[286] and pain in youth.[287]

A number of the practices described here are derived from the ancient system of yoga. Yoga is not a religion. Both yoga and meditation are scientifically associated with a healthy lifestyle, preventative medicine, and health care.[288] They have been popularized in recent decades by medical researchers, psychologists, and others who have rediscovered their benefits. Yoga is a system of powerful tools for achieving union and healing within the individual, with others, and with a higher force. Yoga techniques not only calm the body, but also are a means of healing the sense of isolation that can lead to stress and illness.

Meditation induces physical and mental relaxation. Meditation is associated with neuroplasticity phenomena, reducing age-related brain degeneration and improving cognitive functions[289] due to cognitive restructuring, autonomic changes, and release of cytokines.[290] Meditation has been shown to improve memory in studies of people with subjective cognitive decline, mild cognitive impairment, and highly stressed caregivers, all of whom are at increased risk for subsequent development of Alzheimer's Disease. Kirtan Kriya meditation has been shown to improve sleep, decrease depression, reduce anxiety, down-regulate inflammatory genes, up-regulate immune system genes, improve insulin and glucose regulatory genes, and increase telomerase by 43%.[291]

B. Basic Stress Management Guidelines

a. Daily Practice:

Consistency is one of the most important aspects of developing a personal practice. Stress management relaxation techniques are a form of physical and mental training. They are far more effective when done regularly and correctly. There is no magic to learning how to relax. Training the body to enter a deep, regenerative state takes time. Some people will learn quickly, while others may need more time and individual instruction.

b. Developing a Routine:

Habits, good or bad, are developed over time. If you choose a regular time and place to do your relaxation, you will be creating a habit you soon will look forward to. To help you develop a routine, you may want to keep a relaxation log, which you can fill out briefly before and after each of your relaxation sessions. Keeping a chart for the first several weeks is a useful incentive and allows you to watch your progress.

c. A Safe Place to Relax:

An important part of developing a routine is to create a safe and quiet place to relax. This may mean asking for cooperation from the other people around you, maybe explaining to them that you need to be alone so you can just concentrate on relaxing. Silencing your telephone can help guarantee quiet time alone. Do whatever you think is necessary to ensure you will not be disturbed. Try to keep your special place orderly and full of fresh air so it is always a pleasure to go there.

d. Timing:

The best time to do stress management is an individual decision based on your schedule and lifestyle. It's important to have an empty stomach, so be sure to wait at least an hour after a meal. Many people choose to do relaxation techniques early in the morning to set the tone for the day, or just before dinner. It can also be done after vigorous activity. Another good idea is to perform your relaxation techniques before going to bed, which will help ensure a restful night's sleep.

e. Mental Attitude:

The mental attitude required for relaxation and meditation is different than the mindset required for most task-oriented activities. Sometimes it takes a while to become comfortable with the attitude of "passive attention." *Passive attention* is best described as paying attention to the process, rather than the goal. Do not push yourself or try too hard to concentrate. Rather, let your attention focus on your breathing, an object such as a flower or candle, a pleasant mental picture, or whatever technique you find best. If your mind wanders (and it surely will many times in the course of each exercise), simply finish the thought and then bring your mind back to your object of attention. Do not be critical of yourself or try to keep your mind from wandering. This will only defeat you and may make you tense up while you are trying to relax and meditate.

Do not think about getting relaxed, which is your goal; pay attention to whatever sensation you are having at the moment, no matter what it is. If you find it hard to do the exercise or to relax, pay attention to your body and try to find out why. You may need to change your position, write something down, make a phone call, or finish a task before you are fully ready to relax.

f. Problems and Discomfort:

Because we all have expectations about the benefits of relaxation, many people begin to practice stress management and feel they are not doing it right. It seems too simple! Their experience does not fit their expectations, however vague and unrealistic these expectations may be. Trust yourself.

Sometimes a person will experience some discomfort, either physical tension or anxiety, during or after stress management. This is because in relaxing you may become aware of tension in your body that you had ignored or not even realized you had, or you may be letting feelings or thoughts into conscious awareness that you had previously repressed. In most cases the solution is to wait for a while and then continue the exercise; however, if discomfort or anxiety persists, it is wise to consult with a professional.

C. Meditation How-To

1. Physical Recommendations

- Avoid meditating immediately after a meal. Wait at least one hour.
- For early morning meditations, do a few stretches and splash some cold water on your face to help you fully awaken.
- A straight-backed chair, a firm cushion or pillow or a folded blanket placed under the buttocks helps to make sitting more comfortably.
- Make sure your clothing is comfortable and sufficiently warm (the body will cool down as you relax).
- Meditate in a well-ventilated room.
- Decorate the meditation room with pictures, candles, inspirational books, sacred objects, etc. - anything that would remind you of your purpose in meditation.
- It's best to meditate in the same place, at the same time every day.
- Two sittings daily of 15 to 20 minutes is a good start for meditation practice; sit in the morning when you get up and in the evening before retiring. Very early in the morning (4:00 to 7:00 a.m.) is an especially good time to meditate.
- Breathing practices help to center the mind and relax the body in preparation for meditation.

2. Practical Recommendations

- Meditating regularly is important. It is through regularity that the habit of meditation can be cultivated. Thus, when meditation becomes a habit, "second nature" to you, it will actually be harder for you to skip your meditation than to meditate.
- Don't be anxious or disturbed over distracting thoughts coming into your mind during your sitting. Simply try to ignore them. Know that your intention is meditation — if these thoughts want to sit for a while in your mental "room," that's up to them. Don't try to force them out — you'll create an enemy. Learning to LET GO of these distracting thoughts is a valuable technique.
- Tend to the PROCESS of meditation rather than the goal. If you do it properly, you will get results.
- Sometimes it may seem that your mind is more disturbed in meditation than during other times. Usually this is because you've never been still or quiet enough to notice all the "static" on your mental radio. It's all always been there—it's you! Enjoy the "music"—all the drama, romance, intrigue, comedy—it's all there, in you. Listen to the show as it goes by, but don't get caught up in any of the scenes, no matter how dramatic. Remain as a witness. Use your object of meditation as your anchor.
- If an outside sound—a train whistle, a ringing phone, etc.—enters your mind, notice it and then let it pass through your awareness and gently leave your mind without attaching to it. Do the same thing with thoughts as they enter your mind: notice them, and then allow them to pass through and out of your awareness without attaching to them or letting them kidnap and abduct your mind-state.

- Be loving but firm. Don't make your mind afraid of you. After all, it's just doing the best it can under the circumstances. Let it know WHY you want to meditate.
- Approach your practice with a sense of fun and adventure.
- If possible, be around others who meditate; you will inspire each other.

5. LOVE AND SUPPORT SYSTEMS

Medicine today tends to focus primarily on the physical and mechanistic: drugs and surgery, genes, microbes and molecules. However, there isn't any other factor in medicine—not diet, smoking, exercise, stress, genetics, drugs, or surgery—that has a greater impact on our quality of life, incidence of illness, and premature death from all causes than loneliness and isolation.[292]

Love and intimacy—our ability to connect with ourselves and others—is at the root of what makes us sick and what makes us well, what causes sadness and what brings happiness, what makes us suffer and what leads to healing.[293]

There is a deep spiritual hunger in the world. The profound sense of loneliness, isolation, alienation, and depression that are so prevalent in our culture with the breakdown of the social structures that used to provide us with a sense of connection and community. It is a root of the illness, cynicism, and violence in our society.

We are creatures of community. Awareness is the first step in healing, both individually and socially. Part of the value of science is to increase the level of awareness of how much these choices matter that we make each day. When we understand how important these issues are, then we can do something about it. These include:

- Spending more time with our friends and family
- Improving communication skills
- Building positive group support
- Practicing acceptance, forgiveness, and redemption
- Practicing compassion, altruism, and service
- Seeking psychotherapy
- Practicing touching and other ways of physical contact
- Practicing daily meditation

~ Be Part of the Change ~

By providing people the access to this kind of evidence-based content we can all help break the current paradigm, shake the status quo and change the current corporate-led system. Please invite others to purchase and download this Universal Guideline and support our work. This way we can continue creating vital content that builds thriving individuals who rely on self-sufficiency through educated decisions for true health and wellbeing.

Visit our website at wfpb.org and contribute with donations at www.wfpb.org/donate

REFERENCES

[1] Aleksandrowicz L, Green R, Joy EJM, Smith P, Haines A. The impacts of dietary change on greenhouse gas emissions, land use, water use, and health: a systematic review. PLoS One 2016; 11: e0165797.

[2] Nelson ME, Hamm MW, Hu FB, Abrams SA, Griffin TS. alignment of healthy dietary patterns and environmental sustainability: a systematic review. Adv Nutr An Int Rev J 2016; 7: 1005–25.
[3] Hallström E, Carlsson-Kanyama A, Börjesson P. Environmental impact of dietary change: a systematic review. J Clean Prod 2015; 91: 1–11.

[4] Joyce A, Hallett J, Hannelly T, Carey G. The impact of nutritional choices on global warming and policy implications: examining the link between dietary choices and greenhouse gas emissions. Energy Emiss Control Technol 2014; 2: 33.

[5] Burlingame B, Dernini S, Nutrition and Consumer Protection Division, FAO. Sustainable diets and biodiversity: directions and solutions for policy, research and action. International scientific symposium, biodiversity and sustainable diets united against hunger; Rome, Italy; Nov 3–5, 2010

[6] Payne CL, Scarborough P, Cobiac L. Do low-carbon-emission diets lead to higher nutritional quality and positive health outcomes? A systematic review of the literature. Public Health Nutr 2016; 19: 2654–61

[7] Springmann, Marco, et al. "Analysis and Valuation of the Health and Climate Change Cobenefits of Dietary Change." *PNAS*, National Academy of Sciences, 18 Mar. 2016, www.pnas.org/content/early/2016/03/16/1523119113.

[8] Wang DD, Leung CW, Li Y, et al. Trends in Dietary Quality Among Adults in the United States, 1999 Through 2010. *JAMA Intern Med.* 2014;174(10):1587–1595. doi:10.1001/jamainternmed.2014.3422

[9] Forouzanfar MH, Alexander L, Anderson HR, et al. Global, regional, and national comparative risk assessment of 79 behavioural, environmental and occupational, and metabolic risks or clusters of risks in 188 countries, 1990–2013: a systematic analysis for the Global Burden of Disease Study 2013. Lancet 2015;386: 2287–323.

[10] "The Top 10 Causes of Death." *World Health Organization*, World Health Organization, www.who.int/news-room/fact-sheets/detail/the-top-10-causes-of-death.

[11] Springmann M, Godfray HCJ, Rayner M, Scarborough P. Analysis and valuation of the health and climate change cobenefits of dietary change. Proc Natl Acad Sci 2016; 113: 4146–51.

[12] Lozano R, et al. (2012) Global and regional mortality from 235 causes of death for 20 age groups in 1990 and 2010: A systematic analysis for the Global Burden of Disease Study 2010. Lancet 380(9859):2095–2128.

[13] Tremmel M, Gerdtham UG, Nilsson PM, Saha S. Economic Burden of Obesity: A Systematic Literature Review. Int J Environ Res Public Health. 2017;14(4):435. Published 2017 Apr 19. doi:10.3390/ijerph14040435

[14] Hammond R.A., Levine R. The economic impact of obesity in the United States. Diabetes Metab. Syndr. Obes. 2010;3:285–295. doi: 10.2147/DMSO.S7384.

[15] Tsai A.G., Williamson D.F., Glick H.A. Direct medical cost of overweight and obesity in the USA: A quantitative systematic review. Obes. Rev. 2011;12:50–61. doi: 10.1111/j.1467-789X.2009.00708.x.

[16] Lehnert T., Sonntag D., Konnopka A., Riedel-Heller S., Konig H.H. Economic costs of overweight and obesity. Best Prac. Res. Clin. Endocrinol. Metab. 2013;27:105–115. doi: 10.1016/j.beem.2013.01.002.

[17] Muller-Riemenschneider F., Reinhold T., Berghofer A., Willich S.N. Health-economic burden of obesity in Europe. Eur. J. Epidemiol. 2008;23:499–509. doi: 10.1007/s10654-008-9239-1.

[18] Von Lengerke T., Krauth C. Economic costs of adult obesity: A review of recent European studies with a focus on subgroup-specific costs. Maturitas. 2011;69:220–229. doi: 10.1016/j.maturitas.2011.04.005.

[19] Bahia L., Coutinho E.S., Barufaldi L.A., Abreu Gde A., Malhao T.A., De Souza C.P., Araujo D.V. The costs of overweight and obesity-related diseases in the Brazilian public health system: Cross-sectional study. BMC Public Health. 2012;12 doi: 10.1186/1471-2458-12-440.

[20] Konnopka A., Bodemann M., Konig H.H. Health burden and costs of obesity and overweight in Germany. Eur. J. Health Econ. 2011;12:345–352. doi: 10.1007/s10198-010-0242-6.

[21] Kang J.H., Jeong B.G., Cho Y.G., Song H.R., Kim K.A. Socioeconomic costs of overweight and obesity in Korean adults. J. Korean Med. Sci. 2011;26:1533–1540. doi: 10.3346/jkms.2011.26.12.1533.

[22] Dobbs R., Sawers C., Thompson F., Manyika J., Woetzel J.R., Child P., McKenna S., Spatharou A.Overcoming Obesity: An Initial Economic Analysis. McKinsey Global Institute; Jakarta, Indonesia: 2014.

[23] Worldwide trends in diabetes since 1980: a pooled analysis of 751 population-based studies with 4·4 million participants," NCD Risk Factor Collaboration, *The Lancet*, April 6, 2016, dx.doi.org/10.1016/ S0140-6736(16)00618-8.

24 Global Burden of Metabolic Risk Factors for Chronic Diseases Collaboration. Cardiovascular disease, chronic kidney disease, and diabetes mortality burden of cardiometabolic risk factors from 1980 to 2010: a comparative risk assessment. *Lancet Diabetes Endocrinol.* 2014; 2: 634-647

25 Seuring T., Archangelidi O., Suhrcke M. The economic costs of type 2 diabetes: a global systematic review. *Pharmacoeconomics.* 2015; 33: 811-831

[26] World Health Organization and World Economic Forum . From Burden to "Best Buys": Reducing the Economic Impact of Non-Communicable Diseases in Low- and Middle-Income Countries. Geneva: World Economic Forum; 2011.

[27] Gheorghe A, Griffiths U, Murphy A, Legido-Quigley H, Lamptey P, Perel P. The economic burden of cardiovascular disease and hypertension in low- and middle-income countries: a systematic review. *BMC Public Health.* 2018;18(1):975. Published 2018 Aug 6. doi:10.1186/s12889-018-5806-x

[28] Horrigan L, Lawrence RS, Walker P. How sustainable agriculture can address the environmental and human health harms of industrial agriculture. Environ Health Perspect. 2002;110(5):445-56.

[29] Butler, R. A. (2019, April 9). Amazon Destruction. Retrieved from https://rainforests.mongabay.com/amazon/amazon_destruction.html

[30] Food and Agriculture Organization of the United Nations, International Fund for Agricultural Development, the United Nations Children's Fund, World Food Programme, WHO. The state of food security and nutrition in the world. Geneva: World Health Organization, 2018.

[31] Springmann M, Clark M, Mason-D'Croz D, et al. Options for keeping the food system within environmental limits. Nature 2018; published online Oct 10. DOI:10.1038/s41586-018-0594-0.

[32] Meyer-Abich KM. Human health in nature—towards a holistic philosophy of nutrition. Public Health Nutr 2005;8:738–42

[33] Fardet A, Rock E. Toward a new philosophy of preventive nutrition: from a reductionist to a holistic paradigm to improve nutritional recommendations. Adv Nutr. 2014;5(4):430-46. Published 2014 Jul 7. doi:10.3945/an.114.006122

[34] Fardet A, Rock E. Toward a new philosophy of preventive nutrition: from a reductionist to a holistic paradigm to improve nutritional recommendations. *Adv Nutr.* 2014;5(4):430-46. Published 2014 Jul 7. doi:10.3945/an.114.006122

[35] Fardet A, Rock E. Toward a new philosophy of preventive nutrition: from a reductionist to a holistic paradigm to improve nutritional recommendations. *Adv Nutr.* 2014;5(4):430-46. Published 2014 Jul 7. doi:10.3945/an.114.006122

[36] Fardet A, Rock E. Toward a new philosophy of preventive nutrition: from a reductionist to a holistic paradigm to improve nutritional recommendations. *Adv Nutr.* 2014;5(4):430-46. Published 2014 Jul 7. doi:10.3945/an.114.006122

[37] Campbell, T C, and Howard Jacobson. *Whole: Rethinking the Science of Nutrition.* Dallas, TX: BenBella Books, Inc, 2013. Print.

[38] TC, C. (2019). *Cancer Prevention and Treatment by Wholistic Nutrition. - PubMed - NCBI.* [online] Ncbi.nlm.nih.gov. Available at: https://www.ncbi.nlm.nih.gov/pubmed/29057328 [Accessed 11 Feb. 2019].

[39] Campbell TC. Nutritional Renaissance and Public Health Policy. *J Nutr Biol.* 2017;3(1):124-138.

[40] Campbell TC. Nutritional Renaissance and Public Health Policy. *J Nutr Biol.* 2017;3(1):124-138.

[41] H Trowell. Ischemic heart disease and dietary fiber. Am J Clin Nutr. 1972 Sep;25(9):926-32.

[42] Yu N, Su X, Wang Z, Dai B, Kang J. Association of Dietary Vitamin A and β-Carotene Intake with the Risk of Lung Cancer: A Meta-Analysis of 19 Publications. *Nutrients.* 2015;7(11):9309-24. Published 2015 Nov 11. doi:10.3390/nu7115463

43 I Hoffman. Transcending reductionism in nutrition research. Am J Clin Nutr. 2003 Sep;78(3 Suppl):514S-516S.

44 Y Li, T Zhang. Targeting cancer stem cells with sulforaphane, a dietary component from broccoli and broccoli sprouts. Future Oncol 2013 9(8):1097 - 1103.

45 J A Higgins, I L Brown. Resistant starch: a promising dietary agent for the prevention/treatment of inflammatory bowel disease and bowel cancer. Curr Opin Gastroenterol. 2013 Mar;29(2):190-4.

46 Springmann, Marco, et al. "Analysis and Valuation of the Health and Climate Change Cobenefits of Dietary Change." PNAS, National Academy of Sciences, 12 Apr. 2016, www.pnas.org/content/113/15/4146.

47 Shelton, Herbert M. *The Science and Art of Fasting*. Mockingbird Press, 2019.

48 Shelton, Herbert. *Hygienic System Vol. III - Fasting and Sunbathing*. Health Research, 2005.

49 Campbell, T C. "The Past, Present, and Future of Nutrition and Cancer: Part 1-Was A Nutritional Association Acknowledged a Century Ago?" Nutrition and Cancer., U.S. National Library of Medicine, July 2017, www.ncbi.nlm.nih.gov/pubmed/28594590.

50 Song M, Fung TT, Hu FB, et al. Association of Animal and Plant Protein Intake With All-Cause and Cause-Specific Mortality. *JAMA Intern Med.* 2016;176(10):1453–1463. doi:10.1001/jamainternmed.2016.4182

51 Orlich MJ, Singh PN, Sabaté J, et al. Vegetarian dietary patterns and mortality in Adventist Health Study 2. JAMA Intern Med. 2013 Jul 8;173(13):1230–8. DOI:http://dx.doi.org/10.1001/jamainternmed.2013.6473.

52 Rosell M, Appleby P, Spencer E, Key T. Weight gain over 5 years in 21,966 meat-eating, fish-eating, vegetarian, and vegan men and women in EPIC-Oxford. Int J Obes (Lond) 2006 Sep;30(9):1389–96. DOI:http://dx.doi.org/10.1038/sj.ijo.0803305.

53 Ornish D. Statins and the soul of medicine. Am J Cardiol. 2002 Jun 1;89(11):1286–90. DOI:http://dx.doi.org/10.1016/S0002-9149(02)02327-5.

54 Jenkins DJ, Kendall CW, Marchie A, et al. Direct comparison of a dietary portfolio of cholesterol-lowering foods with a statin in hypercholesterolemic participants. Am J Clin Nutr. 2005 Feb;81(2):380–7.

55 Barnard ND, Cohen J, Jenkins DJ, et al. A low-fat vegan diet and a conventional diabetes diet in the treatment of type 2 diabetes: a randomized, controlled, 74-wk clinical trial. Am J Clin Nutr. 2009 May;89(5):1588S–1596S. DOI: http://dx.doi.org/10.3945/ajcn.2009.26736H.

56 Huang T, Yang B, Zheng J, Li G, Wahlqvist ML, Li D. Cardiovascular disease mortality and cancer incidence in vegetarians: a meta-analysis and systematic review. Ann Nutr Metab. 2012;60(4):233–40.DOI: http://dx.doi.org/10.1159/000337301.

57 Tuso PJ, Ismail MH, Ha BP, Bartolotto C. Nutritional update for physicians: plant-based diets. Perm J. 2013 Spring;17(2):61–6. DOI: http://dx.doi.org/10.7812/TPP/12-085.

58 Tonstad S, Butler T, Yan R, Fraser GE. Type of vegetarian diet, body weight, and prevalence of type 2 diabetes. Diabetes Care. 2009 May;32(5):791–6. DOI: http://dx.doi.org/10.2337/dc08-1886.

59 Berkow SE, Barnard N. Vegetarian diets and weight status. Nutr Rev. 2006 Apr;64(4):175–88. DOI: http://dx.doi.org/10.1111/j.1753-4887.2006.tb00200.x.

60 Farmer B, Larson BT, Fulgoni VL, 3rd, Rainville AJ, Liepa GU. A vegetarian dietary pattern as a nutrient-dense approach to weight management: an analysis of the national health and nutrition examination survey 1999–2004. J Am Diet Assoc. 2011 Jun;111(6):819–27. DOI:http://dx.doi.org/10.1016/j.jada.2011.03.012.

61 Wang Y, Beydoun MA. Meat consumption is associated with obesity and central obesity among US adults. Int J Obes (Lond) 2009 Jun;33(6):621–8. DOI: http://dx.doi.org/10.1038/ijo.2009.45.

62 Rosell M, Appleby P, Spencer E, Key T. Weight gain over 5 years in 21,966 meat-eating, fish-eating, vegetarian, and vegan men and women in EPIC-Oxford. Int J Obes (Lond) 2006 Sep;30(9):1389–96. DOI:http://dx.doi.org/10.1038/sj.ijo.0803305.

63 Tonstad S, Butler T, Yan R, Fraser GE. Type of vegetarian diet, body weight, and prevalence of type 2 diabetes. Diabetes Care. 2009 May;32(5):791 6. DOI: http://dx.doi.org/10.2337/dc08-1886.

[64] Sabaté J, Wien M. Vegetarian diets and childhood obesity prevention. Am J Clin Nutr. 2010 May;91(5):1525S–1529S. DOI: http://dx.doi.org/10.3945/ajcn.2010.28701F.

[65] Report of the Dietary Guidelines Advisory Committee on the dietary guidelines for Americans, 2010: to the Secretary of Agriculture and the Secretary of Health and Human Services. Washington, DC: Agriculture Research Service, US Department of Agriculture, US Department of Health and Human Services; 2010.

[66] Takahashi Y, Sasaki S, Okubo S, Hayashi M, Tsugane S. Blood pressure change in a free-living population-based dietary modification study in Japan. J Hypertens. 2006 Mar;24(3):451–8. DOI: http://dx.doi.org/10.1097/01.hjh.0000209980.36359.16.

[67] Appleby PN, Davey GK, Key TJ. Hypertension and blood pressure among meat eaters, fish eaters, vegetarians and vegans in EPIC-Oxford. Public Health Nutr. 2002 Oct;5(5):645–54. DOI:http://dx.doi.org/10.1079/PHN2002332.

[68] Ferdowsian HR, Barnard ND. Effects of plant-based diets on plasma lipids. Am J Cardiol. 2009 Oct 1;104(7):947–56. DOI: http://dx.doi.org/10.1016/j.amjcard.2009.05.032.

[69] Ferdowsian HR, Barnard ND. Effects of plant-based diets on plasma lipids. Am J Cardiol. 2009 Oct 1;104(7):947–56. DOI: http://dx.doi.org/10.1016/j.amjcard.2009.05.032.

[70] Report of the Dietary Guidelines Advisory Committee on the dietary guidelines for Americans, 2010: to the Secretary of Agriculture and the Secretary of Health and Human Services. Washington, DC: Agriculture Research Service, US Department of Agriculture, US Department of Health and Human Services; 2010.

[71] Singh PN, Sabaté J, Fraser GE. Does low meat consumption increase life expectancy in humans? Am J Clin Nutr. 2003 Sep;78(3 Suppl):526S–532S.

[72] Campbell TC, Campbell TM., II . The China study: the most comprehensive study of nutrition ever conducted and the startling implications for diet, weight loss and long-term health. Dallas, TX: BenBella Books; 2006.

[73] Sinha R, Cross AJ, Graubard BI, Leitzmann MF, Schatzkin A. Meat intake and mortality: a prospective study of over half a million people. Arch Intern Med. 2009 Mar 23;169(6):562–71. DOI: http://dx.doi.org/10.1001/archinternmed.2009.6.

[74] Huang T, Yang B, Zheng J, Li G, Wahlqvist ML, Li D. Cardiovascular disease mortality and cancer incidence in vegetarians: a meta-analysis and systematic review. Ann Nutr Metab. 2012;60(4):233–40.DOI: http://dx.doi.org/10.1159/000337301.

[75] TC, C. (2019). *Cancer Prevention and Treatment by Wholistic Nutrition. - PubMed - NCBI.* [online] Ncbi.nlm.nih.gov. Available at: https://www.ncbi.nlm.nih.gov/pubmed/29057328 [Accessed 11 Feb. 2019].

[76] Ornish D, Scherwitz LW, Billings JH, et al. Intensive lifestyle changes for reversal of coronary heart disease. JAMA. 1998 Dec 16;280(23):2001–7. DOI: http://dx.doi.org/10.1001/jama.280.23.2001.

[77] Esselstyn CB, Jr, Gendy G, Doyle J, Golubic M, Roizen MF. A way to reverse CAD? J Fam Pract. 2014 Jul;63(7):356–364b.

[78] Freeman, A M, et al. "Trending Cardiovascular Nutrition Controversies." Journal of the American College of Cardiology., U.S. National Library of Medicine, 7 Mar. 2017, www.ncbi.nlm.nih.gov/pubmed/28254181.

[79] Ornish D, Brown SE, Scherwitz LW, et al. Can lifestyle changes reverse coronary heart disease? The Lifestyle Heart Trial. Lancet. 1990 Jul 21;336(8708):129–33. DOI: http://dx.doi.org/10.1016/0140-6736(90)91656-U.

[80] Ornish D, Scherwitz LW, Billings JH, et al. Intensive lifestyle changes for reversal of coronary heart disease. JAMA. 1998 Dec 16;280(23):2001–7. DOI: http://dx.doi.org/10.1001/jama.280.23.2001.

[81] de Lorgeril M, Salen P, Martin JL, Monjaud I, Delaye J, Mamelle N. Mediterranean diet, traditional risk factors, and the rate of cardiovascular complications after myocardial infarction: final report of the Lyon Diet Heart Study. Circulation. 1999 Feb;99(6):779–85. DOI:http://dx.doi.org/10.1161/01.CIR.99.6.779.

[82] Key TJ, Fraser GE, Thorogood M, et al. Mortality in vegetarians and non-vegetarians: a collaborative analysis of 8300 deaths among 76,000 men and women in five prospective studies. Public Health Nutr. 1998 Mar;1(1):33–41. DOI: http://dx.doi.org/10.1079/PHN19980006.

[83] Appleby PN, Thorogood M, McPherson K, Mann JI. Associations between plasma lipid concentrations and dietary, lifestyle and physical factors in the Oxford Vegetarian Study. J Hum Nutr Diet. 1995 Oct;8(5):305–14. DOI: http://dx.doi.org/10.1111/j.1365-277X.1995.tb00324.x.

[84] Fraser GE. Vegetarian diets: what do we know of their effects on common chronic diseases? Am J Clin Nutr. 2009;89(5):1607S–1612S. DOI: http://dx.doi.org/10.3945/ajcn.2009.26736K Erratum in: Am J Clin Nutr 2009 Jul;90(1):248. DOI: http://dx.doi.org/10.3945/ajcn.2009.27933.

[85] Campbell, T. (2019). *A plant-based diet and animal protein: questioning dietary fat and considering animal protein as the main cause of heart disease.* [online] PubMed Central (PMC). Available at: https://www.ncbi.nlm.nih.gov/pmc/articles/PMC5466939/ [Accessed 11 Feb. 2019].

[86] Snowdon DA, Phillips RL. Does a vegetarian diet reduce the occurrence of diabetes? Am J Public Health. 1985 May;75(5):507–12. DOI: http://dx.doi.org/10.2105/AJPH.75.5.507.

[87] Vang A, Singh PN, Lee JW, Haddad EH, Brinegar CH. Meats, processed meats, obesity, weight gain and occurrence of diabetes among adults: findings from Adventist Health Studies. Ann Nutr Metab. 2008;52(2):96–104. DOI: http://dx.doi.org/10.1159/000121365.

[88] Barnard ND, Cohen J, Jenkins DJ, et al. A low-fat vegan diet improves glycemic control and cardiovascular risk factors in a randomized clinical trial in individuals with type 2 diabetes. Diabetes Care. 2006 Aug;29(8):1777–83. DOI: http://dx.doi.org/10.2337/dc06-0606.

[89] D. Harman Aging: A theory based on free radical and radiation chemistry J Gerontol, 11 (1956), pp. 298-300.

[90] H. Sies Oxidative stress: oxidants and antioxidants Exp Physiol, 82 (1997), pp. 291-295

[91] T. Heitzer, T. Schlinzig, K. Krohn, et al. Endothelial dysfunction, oxidative stress, and risk of cardiovascular events in patients with coronary artery disease Circulation, 104 (2001), pp. 2673-2678.

[92] S. Reuter, S.C. Gupta, M.M. Chaturvedi, et al. Oxidative stress, inflammation, and cancer: how are they linked? Free Radic Biol Med, 49 (2010), pp. 1603-1616

[93] C.J. Wruck, A. Fragoulis, A. Gurzynski, et al. Role of oxidative stress in rheumatoid arthritis: insights from the Nrf2-knockout mice Ann Rheum Dis, 70 (2011), pp. 844-850

[94] J.S. Moylan, M.B. Reid Oxidative stress, chronic disease, and muscle wasting Muscle Nerve, 35 (2007), pp. 411-429

[95] G. Perry, A.D. Cash, M. Smith Alzheimer disease and oxidative stress J Biomed Biotechnol, 2 (2002), pp. 120-123

[96] P. Jenner Oxidative stress in Parkinson's disease Ann Neurol, 53 Suppl 3 (2003), pp. S26-S36
discussion S36–8

[97] Egger, Garry, et al. "Introduction to the Role of Lifestyle Factors in Medicine." Introduction to the Role of Lifestyle Factors in Medicine - ScienceDirect, Academic Press, 24 Mar. 2017,

[98] Blaney D, Diehl H. The optimal diet: the official CHIP cookbook. Hagerstown, MD: Autumn House Publishing; 2009. Jan 1,

[99] McDougall JA, McDougall M. The new McDougall cookbook: 300 delicious ultra-low-fat recipes. New York, NY: Plume; 1997. Jan 1, 1997.

[100] The Cambridge World History of Food, Volume 2 - University of Cambridge - Cambridge University Press, 2000

[101] Engelhardt, Ute (2001), "Dietetics in Tang China and the first extant works of material dietetica", in Elisabeth Hsü (ed.), Innovation in Chinese Medicine, Cambridge: Cambridge University Press, pp. 173–191, ISBN 0-521-80068-4.

[102] Benn, Charles. (2002). China's Golden Age: Everyday Life in the Tang Dynasty. Oxford University Press. ISBN 0-19-517665-0.p. 122

[103] Barnes, Linda L. (2013), "A World of Chinese Medicine and Healing: Part Two", in TJ Hinrichs and Linda L. Barnes (eds.), Chinese Medicine and Healing: An Illustrated History, Cambridge, Mass.: The Belknap Press of Harvard University Press, pp. 334–378, ISBN 978-0-674-04737-2.

[104] The Cultural History of Plants - Sir Ghillean Prance, Mark Nesbitt - Routledge, Oct 12, 2012

[105] Mt. Pleasant, Jane (2006). "The science behind the Three Sisters mound system: An agronomic assessment of an indigenous agricultural system in the northeast". In John E. Staller, Robert H. Tykot, and Bruce F. Benz. Histories of maize: Multidisciplinary approaches to the prehistory, linguistics, biogeography, domestication, and evolution of maize. Amsterdam. pp. 529–537.

---

[106] Bronson, Bennet (1966). "Roots and the Subsistence of the Ancient Maya". Southwestern Journal of Anthropology 22: 251–279.

[107] Arnot, Bob, The Aztec Diet: Chia Power: The Superfood that Gets You Skinny and Keeps You Healthy - Harper Collins, 2013

[108] Smith, Michael Ernest, The Aztecs, Wiley Blackwell, 2nd ed. 2002, ISBN 978-0631230168

[109] The Aztecs - Michael E. Smith - John Wiley & Sons, Mar 1, 2013

[110] Food in the Ancient World - Joan Pilsbury Alcock - Greenwood Publishing Group, 2006

[111] The Cambridge World History of Food, Volume 2 - University of Cambridge - Cambridge University Press, 2000

[112] Tuso PJ, Ismail MH, Ha BP, Bartolotto C. Nutritional update for physicians: plant-based diets. Perm J. 2013;17(2):61-6.

[113] E. Ros. Health benefits of nut consumption. Nutrients, 2 (2010), pp. 652-682

[114] Afshin, Ashkan, et al. "Consumption of Nuts and Legumes and Risk of Incident Ischemic Heart Disease, Stroke, and Diabetes: a Systematic Review and Meta-Analysis." OUP Academic, Oxford University Press, 4 June 2014, academic.oup.com/ajcn/article/100/1/278/4576571.

[115] E. Viguiliouk, C.W. Kendall, S. Blanco Mejia, et al. Effect of tree nuts on glycemic control in diabetes: a systematic review and meta-analysis of randomized controlled dietary trials

[116] D. Zhou, H. Yu, F. He, et al. Nut consumption in relation to cardiovascular disease risk and type-2 diabetes: a systematic review and meta-analysis of prospective studies. Am J Clin Nutr, 100 (2014), pp. 270-277

[117] J. Sabaté, K. Oda, E. Ros Nut consumption and blood lipids: a pooled analysis of 25 intervention trials. Arch Intern Med, 170 (2010), pp. 821-827

[118] J. Salas-Salvadó, J. Fernández-Ballart, E.Ros, et al., PREDIMED Study Investigators. Effect of the Mediterranean diet supplemented with nuts on metabolic syndrome status: one-year results of the PREDIMED randomized trial. Arch Intern Med, 168 (2008), pp. 2449- 2458

[119] N. Babio, E. Toledo, R. Estruch, et al., PREDIMED Study Investigators Mediterranean diets and metabolic syndrome status in the PREDIMED randomized trial. CMAJ, 186 (2014), pp. E649-E657

[120] N. Babio, E. Toledo, R. Estruch, et al., PREDIMED Study Investigators Mediterranean diets and metabolic syndrome status in the PREDIMED randomized trial. CMAJ, 186 (2014), pp. E649-E657

[121] Liong M.-T. (2010) Cholesterol-lowering effects of probiotics and prebiotics: a review of in vivo and in vitro findings. Int J Mol Sci 11:2499–2522.

[122] Jones M.L., Martoni C.J., Prakash S. (2012) Cholesterol lowering and inhibition of sterol absorption by lactobacillus reuteri ncimb 30242: a randomized controlled trial. Eur J Clin Nutr 66:1234–1241.

[123] Jamilian, Mehri, et al. "Effects of Probiotic Supplementation on Metabolic Status in Pregnant Women: a Randomized, Double-Blind, Placebo-Controlled Trial." *Archives of Iranian Medicine*, U.S. National Library of Medicine, Oct. 2016, www.ncbi.nlm.nih.gov/pubmed/27743432.

[124] Akkasheh, Ghodarz, et al. "Clinical and Metabolic Response to Probiotic Administration in Patients with Major Depressive Disorder: A Randomized, Double-Blind, Placebo-Controlled Trial." *Nutrition (Burbank, Los Angeles County, Calif.)*, U.S. National Library of Medicine, Mar. 2016, www.ncbi.nlm.nih.gov/pubmed/26706022.

[125] Zamani, Batol, et al. "Clinical and Metabolic Response to Probiotic Supplementation in Patients with Rheumatoid Arthritis: a Randomized, Double-Blind, Placebo-Controlled Trial." *International Journal of Rheumatic Diseases*, U.S. National Library of Medicine, Sept. 2016, www.ncbi.nlm.nih.gov/pubmed/27135916.

[126] Badehnoosh, Bita, et al. "The Effects of Probiotic Supplementation on Biomarkers of Inflammation, Oxidative Stress and Pregnancy Outcomes in Gestational Diabetes." *The Journal of Maternal-Fetal & Neonatal Medicine : the Official Journal of the European Association of Perinatal Medicine, the Federation of Asia and Oceania Perinatal Societies, the International Society of Perinatal Obstetricians*, U.S. National Library of Medicine, May 2018, www.ncbi.nlm.nih.gov/pubmed/28326881.

[127] Ranadheera R.D., Bains S.K., Adams M.C. Importance of food in probiotic efficacy. Food Res. Int. 2010;43:1–7. doi: 10.1016/j.foodres.2009.09.009

[128] Choi I.H., Noh J.S., Han J.S., Kim H.J., Han E.S., Song Y.O. (2013) Kimchi, a fermented vegetable, improves serum lipid profiles in healthy young adults: randomized clinical trial. J Med Food 16:223–229.

[129] Wan-Loy C., Siew-Moi P. (2016) Marine algae as a potential source for anti-obesity agents. Mar Drugs 14:222.

[130] Serban M.C., Sahebkar A., Dragan S., et al. (2016) A systematic review and meta-analysis of the impact of spirulina supplementation on plasma lipid concentrations. Clin Nutr 35:842–851.

[131] Duffy S.J., Keaney J.F. Jr.., Holbrook M., et al. (2001) Short- and long-term black tea consumption reverses endothelial dysfunction in patients with coronary artery disease. Circulation 104:151–156.

[132] Li X., Yu C., Guo Y., et al. (2017) Tea consumption and risk of ischaemic heart disease. Heart 103:783–789.

[133] Kuriyama S., Shimazu T., Ohmori K., et al. (2006) Green tea consumption and mortality due to cardiovascular disease, cancer, and all causes in Japan: The Ohsaki study. JAMA 296:1255–1265.

[134] Bahorun T., Luximon-Ramma A., Neergheen-Bhujun V.S., et al. (2012) The effect of black tea on risk factors of cardiovascular disease in a normal population. Prev Med 54 Suppl:S98–S102.

[135] E. Paterson, M.H. Gordon, C. Niwat, et al.Supplementation with fruit and vegetable soups and beverages increases plasma carotenoid concentrations but does not alter markers of oxidative stress or cardiovascular risk factors J Nutr, 136 (2006), pp. 2849-2855

[136] T.W. George, S. Waroonphan, C. Niwat, et al.Effects of acute consumption of a fruit and vegetable purée-based drink on vasodilation and oxidative status Br J Nutr, 109 (2013), pp. 1442-1452

[137] Sheiham A, James WP. A reappraisal of the quantitative relationship between sugar intake and dental caries: the need for new criteria for developing goals for sugar intake. BMC Public Health. 2014; 14:863 (http://www.ncbi.nlm.nih.gov/pubmed/25228012, accessed 17 January 2015).

[138] Sheiham A, James WP. A new understanding of the relationship between sugars, dental caries and fluoride use: implications for limits on sugars consumption. Public Health Nutr. 2014:1–9 (http://www.ncbi.nlm.nih.gov/pubmed/24892213, accessed 17 January 2015).

[139] Broadbent JM, Thomson WM, Poulton R. Trajectory patterns of dental caries experience in the permanent dentition to the fourth decade of life. J. Dent. Res. 2008; 87(1):69–72 (http://www.ncbi.nlm.nih.gov/pubmed/18096897, accessed 17 January 2015).

[140] Broadbent JM, Foster Page LA, Thomson WM, Poulton R. Permanent dentition caries through the first half of life. Br. Dent. J. 2013; 215(7):E12 (http://www.ncbi.nlm.nih.gov/pubmed/24113990, accessed 17 January 2015).

[141] Horrigan, Leo, et al. "How Sustainable Agriculture Can Address the Environmental and Human Health Harms of Industrial Agriculture." Environmental Health Perspectives, vol. 110, no. 5, 2002, pp. 445–456., doi:10.1289/ehp.02110445

[142] Li Y., Hruby A., Bernstein A.M., et al. (2015) Saturated fats compared with unsaturated fats and sources of carbohydrates in relation to risk of coronary heart disease: a prospective cohort study. J Am Coll Cardiol 66:1538–1548

[143] Dietary Reference Intakes for Water, Potassium, Sodium, Chloride, and Sulfate. (2005). doi:10.17226/10925

[144] U.S. Department of Health and Human Services and U.S. Department of Agriculture. 2015 – 2020 Dietary Guidelines for Americans. 8th ed Washington, DC: U.S. Government Printing Office; (2015).

[145] U.K. National Health Service. Salt: The Facts. Daily salt recommendations for adults. https://www.nhs.uk/live-well/eat-well/salt-nutrition/

[146] K.E. Lundin, C. WijmengaCoeliac disease and autoimmune disease-genetic overlap and screening Nat Rev Gastroenterol Hepatol, 12 (2015), pp. 507-515

[147] Ornish Lifestyle Medicine Program, Ornish.com

[148] Ornish Lifestyle Medicine Program, Ornish.com

[149] Song M, Fung TT, Hu FB, et al. Association of Animal and Plant Protein Intake With All-Cause and Cause-Specific Mortality. *JAMA Intern Med.* 2016;176(10):1453–1463. doi:10.1001/jamainternmed.2016.4182

[150] Battaglia Richi, E., Baumer, B., Conrad, B., Darioli, R., Schmid, A., & Keller, U. (2015). Health Risks Associated with Meat Consumption: A Review of Epidemiological Studies.

[151] Richman, E L, et al. "Intakes of Meat, Fish, Poultry, and Eggs and Risk of Prostate Cancer Progression." Current Neurology and Neuroscience Reports., U.S. National Library of Medicine, Mar. 2010, www.ncbi.nlm.nih.gov/pubmed/20042525.

[152] Friedrich MJ. Processed Meat Consumption Associated With Increased Cancer Risk. *JAMA.*2015;314(23):2496. doi:10.1001/jama.2015.16382

[153] Red and Processed Meat Consumption and Risk of Incident Coronary Heart Disease, Stroke, and Diabetes Mellitus. (n.d.). Retrieved from https://www.ahajournals.org/doi/full/10.1161/circulationaha.109.924977

[154] "Red Meat Consumption and Risk of Stroke." *Stroke*, www.ahajournals.org/doi/full/10.1161/STROKEAHA.112.663286.

[155] Pan A, Sun Q, Bernstein AM, et al. Red meat consumption and mortality: results from 2 prospective cohort studies. *Arch Intern Med.* 2012;172(7):555-63.

[156] Rice BH. Dairy and Cardiovascular Disease: A Review of Recent Observational Research. *Curr Nutr Rep.* 2014;3(2):130-138. Published 2014 Mar 15. doi:10.1007/s13668-014-0076-4

[157] Guo J, Astrup A, Lovegrove JA, Gijsbers L, Givens DI, Soedamah-Muthu SS. Milk and dairy consumption and risk of cardiovascular diseases and all-cause mortality: dose-response meta-analysis of prospective cohort studies. *Eur J Epidemiol.* 2017;32(4):269-287.

[158] Weggemans R.M., Zock P.L., Katan M. (2001) Dietary cholesterol from eggs increase the ratio of total cholesterol to high-density lipoprotein cholesterol in humans: a meta-analysis. Am J Clin Nutr 73:885–891.

[159] Berger S., Raman G., Vishwanathan R., et al. (2015) Dietary cholesterol and cardiovascular disease: A systematic review and meta-analysis. Am J Clin Nutr 102:276–294.

[160] Richman, E L, et al. "Intakes of Meat, Fish, Poultry, and Eggs and Risk of Prostate Cancer Progression." Current Neurology and Neuroscience Reports., U.S. National Library of Medicine, Mar. 2010, www.ncbi.nlm.nih.gov/pubmed/20042525.

[161] Zhong VW, Van Horn L, Cornelis MC, et al. Associations of Dietary Cholesterol or Egg Consumption With Incident Cardiovascular Disease and Mortality. *JAMA.* 2019;321(11):1081–1095. doi:10.1001/jama.2019.1572

[162] D.D. Wang, Y. Li, S.E. Chiuve, M.J. Stampfer, et al.Association of specific dietary fats with total and cause-specific mortality JAMA Intern Med, 176 (2016), pp. 1134-1145

[163] Sun Y., Neelakantan N., Wu Y., et al. (2015) Palm oil consumption increases LDL cholesterol compared with vegetable oils low in saturated fat in a meta-analysis of clinical trials. J Nutr 145:1549–1558.

[164] Eyres L., Eyres M.F., Chisholm A., et al. (2016) Coconut oil consumption and cardiovascular risk factors in humans. Nutr Rev 74:267–280.

[165] Higgins J.P., Tuttle T.D., Higgins C.L. (2010) Energy beverages: content and safety. Mayo Clin Proc 85:1033–1041.

[166] Seifert S.M., Schaechter J.L., Hershorin E.R., Lipshultz S.E. (2011) Health effects of energy drinks on children, adolescents, and young adults. Pediatrics 127:511–528.

[167] Somogyi L.P. (2010) Caffeine Intake by the U.S. Population. Report Prepared for the Food and Drug Administration (Oakridge National Laboratory, Kensington, California).

[168] Cao Y., Willett W.C., Rimm E.B., Stampfer M.J., Giovannucci E.L. (2015) Light to moderate intake of alcohol, drinking patterns, and risk of cancer: results from two prospective US cohort studies. BMJ 351:h4238.

[169] Melina V, Craig W, Levin S. Position of the Academy of Nutrition and Dietetics: Vegetarian Diets. J Acad Nutr Diet. 2016;116:1970–1980.

[170] Farmer B, Larson BT, Fulgoni VL, et al. A vegetarian dietary pattern as a nutrient-dense approach to weight management: an analysis of the national health and nutrition examination survey 1999–2004. J Acad Nutr Diet. 2011;111:819–827.

[171] Campbell, T C. "Untold Nutrition." *Nutrition and Cancer.*, U.S. National Library of Medicine, 2014, www.ncbi.nlm.nih.gov/pubmed/25036857.

[172] Hoffmann, I. "Transcending Reductionism in Nutrition Research." *The American Journal of Clinical Nutrition.*, U.S. National Library of Medicine, Sept. 2003, www.ncbi.nlm.nih.gov/pubmed/12936942.

[173] Campbell, T C. "Cancer Prevention and Treatment by Wholistic Nutrition." *Journal of Nature and Science.*, U.S. National Library of Medicine, Oct. 2017, www.ncbi.nlm.nih.gov/pubmed/29057328.

[174] Freeman, A M, et al. "Trending Cardiovascular Nutrition Controversies." Journal of the American College of Cardiology., U.S. National Library of Medicine, 7 Mar. 2017, www.ncbi.nlm.nih.gov/pubmed/28254181.

[175] United States Department of Agriculture, Agriculture Research Service. USDA Nutrient Database for Standard Reference, Release 14. 2001. Available at: http://www.ars.usda.gov/Services/docs.htm?docid=21215. Accessed January 5, 2017.

[176] Position of the American Dietetic Association: vegetarian diets J Am Diet Assoc, 109 (2009), pp. 1266-1282

[177] Hever J, Cronise RJ. Plant-based nutrition for healthcare professionals: implementing diet as a primary modality in the prevention and treatment of chronic disease.

[178] J Geriatr Cardiol. 2017;14(5):355-368.

[179] Shelton, Herbert M. *The Science and Art of Fasting*. Mockingbird Press, 2019.

[180] Shelton, Herbert M. *The Science and Art of Fasting*. Mockingbird Press, 2019.

[181] Maughan RJ, Fallah J, Coyle EF. The effects of fasting on metabolism and performance. *Br J Sports Med.* 2010;44(7):490-494. doi:10.1136/bjsm.2010.072181

[182] Trepanowski JF, Bloomer RJ. The impact of religious fasting on human health. *Nutr J.* 2010;9:57. Published 2010 Nov 22. doi:10.1186/1475-2891-9-57

[183] Shelton, Herbert M. *The Science and Art of Fasting*. Mockingbird Press, 2019.

[184] Link, Rachael. "8 Health Benefits of Fasting, Backed by Science." *Healthline*, Healthline Media, 22 Nov. 2022, https://www.healthline.com/nutrition/fasting-benefits.

[185] Shelton, Herbert M. *The Science and Art of Fasting*. Mockingbird Press, 2019.

[186] Finnell JS, Saul BC, Goldhamer AC, Myers TR. Is fasting safe? A chart review of adverse events during medically supervised, water-only fasting. *BMC Complement Altern Med.* 2018;18(1):67. Published 2018 Feb 20. doi:10.1186/s12906-018-2136-6

[187] Fredericks R. Fasting: an exceptional human experience. San Jose: All Things Published Well; 2013.

[188] Goldhamer AC, Helms S, Salloum TK. Fasting. 4. St. Louis: Elsevier Churchill Livingstone; 2013.

[189] Furhman J. Fasting and eating for health: a medical doctor's program for conquering disease. New York: St. Martin's Griffin; 1995.

[190] Longo VD, Mattson MP. Fasting: molecular mechanisms and clinical applications. Cell Metab. 2014;19(2):181–192. doi: 10.1016/j.cmet.2013.12.008.

[191] Goldhamer A, Lisle D, Parpia B, Anderson SV, Campbell TC. Medically supervised water-only fasting in the treatment of hypertension. J Manip Physiol Ther. 2001;24(5):335–339. doi: 10.1067/mmt.2001.115263.

[192] Goldhamer AC, Lisle DJ, Sultana P, Anderson SV, Parpia B, Hughes B, Campbell TC. Medically supervised water-only fasting in the treatment of borderline hypertension. J Altern Complement Med. 2002;8(5):643–650. doi: 10.1089/107555302320825165.

[193] Kjeldsen-Kragh J, Haugen M, Borchgrevink CF, Laerum E, Eek M, Mowinkel P, Hovi K, Forre O. Controlled trial of fasting and one-year vegetarian diet in rheumatoid arthritis. Lancet. 1991;338(8772):899–902. doi: 10.1016/0140-6736(91)91770-U.

[194] Horne BD, May HT, Anderson JL, Kfoury AG, Bailey BM, McClure BS, Renlund DG, Lappe DL, Carlquist JF, Fisher PW, et al. Usefulness of routine periodic fasting to lower risk of coronary artery disease in patients undergoing coronary angiography. Am J Cardiol. 2008;102(7):814–819. doi: 10.1016/j.amjcard.2008.05.021.

[195] Horne BD, Muhlestein JB, Lappe DL, May HT, Carlquist JF, Galenko O, Brunisholz KD, Anderson JL. Randomized cross-over trial of short-term water-only fasting: metabolic and cardiovascular consequences. Nutr Metab Cardiovasc Dis. 2013;23(11):1050–1057. doi: 10.1016/j.numecd.2012.09.007

[196] Li C, Ostermann T, Hardt M, Ludtke R, Broecker-Preuss M, Dobos G, Michalsen A. Metabolic and psychological response to 7-day fasting in obese patients with and without metabolic syndrome. Forsch Komplementmed. 2013;20(6):413–420. doi: 10.1159/000353672.

[197] Steiniger J, Schneider A, Bergmann S, Boschmann M, Janietz K. Effects of fasting and endurance training on energy metabolism and physical fitness in obese patients. Forsch Komplementmed. 2009;16(6):383–390. doi: 10.1159/000258142.

[198] Schmidt S, Stange R, Lischka E, Kiehntopf M, Deufel T, Loth D, Uhlemann C. Uncontrolled clinical study of the efficacy of ambulant fasting in patients with osteoarthritis. Forsch Komplementmed. 2010;17(2):87–94. doi: 10.1159/000285479.

[199] Michalsen A, Li C, Kaiser K, Ludtke R, Meier L, Stange R, Kessler C. In-patient treatment of fibromyalgia: a controlled nonrandomized comparison of conventional medicine versus integrative medicine including fasting therapy. Evid Based Complement Alternat Med. 2013;2013:908610

[200] Michalsen A, Kuhlmann MK, Ludtke R, Backer M, Langhorst J, Dobos GJ. Prolonged fasting in patients with chronic pain syndromes leads to late mood-enhancement not related to weight loss and fasting-induced leptin depletion. Nutr Neurosci. 2006;9(5–6):195–200. doi: 10.1080/10284150600929656.

[201] Michalsen A, Hoffmann B, Moebus S, Backer M, Langhorst J, Dobos GJ. Incorporation of fasting therapy in an integrative medicine ward: evaluation of outcome, safety, and effects on lifestyle adherence in a large prospective cohort study. J Altern Complement Med. 2005;11(4):601–607. doi: 10.1089/acm.2005.11.601.

[202] Intermountain Medical Center. "Routine periodic fasting is good for your health, and your heart, study suggests." ScienceDaily. ScienceDaily, 20 May 2011. <www.sciencedaily.com/releases/2011/04/110403090259.htm>.

[203] Goldhamer, Alan C, et al. "Water-Only Fasting and an Exclusively Plant Foods Diet in the Management of Stage IIIa, Low-Grade Follicular Lymphoma." *BMJ Case Reports*, BMJ Publishing Group, 10 Dec. 2015, casereports.bmj.com/content/2015/bcr-2015-211582.long.

[204] Boden G, Chen X, Mozzoli M, *et al.* Effect of fasting on serum leptin in normal human subjects. *J Clin Endocrinol Metab* 1996;81:3419–23.doi:10.1210/jcem.81.9.8784108

[205] Katz LE, DeLeón DD, Zhao H, *et al.* Free and total insulin-like growth factor (IGF)-I levels decline during fasting: relationships with insulin and IGF-binding protein-1. *J Clin Endocrinol Metab* 2002;87:2978–83.doi:10.1210/jcem.87.6.8601

[206] Wilhelmi de Toledo F, Grundler F, Sirtori CR, Ruscica M. Unravelling the health effects of fasting: a long road from obesity treatment to healthy life span increase and improved cognition. *Ann Med.* 2020;52(5):147-161. doi:10.1080/07853890.2020.1770849

[207] Gudden J, Arias Vasquez A, Bloemendaal M. The Effects of Intermittent Fasting on Brain and Cognitive Function. *Nutrients.* 2021;13(9):3166. Published 2021 Sep 10. doi:10.3390/nu13093166

[208] Varady KA, Cienfuegos S, Ezpeleta M, Gabel K. Cardiometabolic Benefits of Intermittent Fasting. *Annu Rev Nutr.* 2021;41:333-361. doi:10.1146/annurev-nutr-052020-041327

[209] Seidler K, Barrow M. Intermittent fasting and cognitive performance - Targeting BDNF as potential strategy to optimise brain health. *Front Neuroendocrinol.* 2022;65:100971. doi:10.1016/j.yfrne.2021.100971

[210] Clifton KK, Ma CX, Fontana L, Peterson LL. Intermittent fasting in the prevention and treatment of cancer. *CA Cancer J Clin.* 2021;71(6):527-546. doi:10.3322/caac.21694

[211] Zhang J, Deng Y, Khoo BL. Fasting to enhance Cancer treatment in models: the next steps. J Biomed Sci. 2020 May 5;27(1):58. doi: 10.1186/s12929-020-00651-0. PMID: 32370764; PMCID: PMC7201989.

[212] Sadeghian M, Rahmani S, Khalesi S, Hejazi E. A review of fasting effects on the response of cancer to chemotherapy. *Clin Nutr.* 2021;40(4):1669-1681. doi:10.1016/j.clnu.2020.10.037

[213] Brandhorst S, Longo VD. Fasting and Caloric Restriction in Cancer Prevention and Treatment. *Recent Results Cancer Res.* 2016;207:241-266. doi:10.1007/978-3-319-42118-6_12

[214] Black, L. J., Lucas, R. M., Sherriff, J. L., Björn, L. O., & Bornman, J. F. (2017). In Pursuit of Vitamin D in Plants. *Nutrients*, *9*(2), 136. http://doi.org/10.3390/nu9020136

[215] Institute of Medicine, Food and Nutrition Board. Dietary Reference Intakes for Calcium and Vitamin D. Washington, DC: National Academy Press, 2010

[216] Optimum Nutrition Recommendations, Michael Greger M.D. FACLM , NutritionFacts.org

[217] Plant-Based Diets: A Physician's Guide. *Perm J.* 2016;20(3):93-101.

[218] Bor MV, von Castel-Roberts KM, Kauwell GP, Stabler SP, Allen RH, Maneval DR, Bailey LB, Nexo E. Daily intake of 4 to 7 mcg dietary vitamin B-12 is associated with steady concentrations of vitamin B-12-related biomarkers in a healthy young population. *Am J Clin Nutr.* 2010;91(3):571-7.

[219] Klee, GG. Cobalamin and folate evaluation: measurement of methylmalonic acid and homocysteine vs vitamin B(12) and folate. *Clin Chem.* 2000; 46 (8): 1277-1283.

[220] Institute of Medicine (US) Standing Committee on the Scientific Evaluation of Dietary Reference Intakes and its Panel on Folate, Other B Vitamins, and Choline (1998) Dietary Reference Intakes for Thiamin, Riboflavin, Niacin, Vitamin B6, Folate, Vitamin B12, Pantothenic Acid, Biotin, and Choline (National Academies Press, Washington, DC).

[221] https://www.ncbi.nlm.nih.gov/books/n/nap6015/appp/def-item/appp.gl1-d19/

[222] https://www.ncbi.nlm.nih.gov/books/n/nap6015/appp/def-item/appp.gl1-d62/

[223] Locatelli, J, et al. "Calcium Handling Proteins: Structure, Function, and Modulation by Exercise." *Current Neurology and Neuroscience Reports.*, U.S. National Library of Medicine, Mar. 2014, www.ncbi.nlm.nih.gov/pubmed/23436107.

[224] Bajaj JK, Salwan P, Salwan S. Various Possible Toxicants Involved in Thyroid Dysfunction: A Review. *J Clin Diagn Res.* 2016;10(1):FE01-3.

[225] "Scientific Opinion on Dietary Reference Values for Iodine." *EFSA Journal*, John Wiley & Sons, Ltd, 7 May 2014, efsa.onlinelibrary.wiley.com/doi/10.2903/j.efsa.2014.3660.

[226] Trumbo P, Yates AA, Schlicker S, et al. Dietary reference intakes: vitamin A, vitamin K, arsenic, boron, chromium, copper, iodine, iron, manganese, molybdenum, nickel, silicon, vanadium, and zinc. J Am Diet Assoc. 2001;101:294–301.

[227] Tadi K, Chang Y, Ashok BT, et al. 3,3'-Diindolylmethane, a cruciferous vegetable derived synthetic anti-proliferative compound in thyroid disease. *Biochem Biophys Res Commun.*2005;337(3):1019-25.

[228] Leung AM, LaMar A, He X, et al. Iodine status and thyroid function of Boston-area vegetarians and vegans. J Clin Endocrinol Metab. 2011,96.E1303–E1307.

[229] Optimum Nutrition Recommendations, Michael Greger M.D. FACLM , NutritionFacts.org

[230] Nagai, M., Hoshide, S., & Kario, K. (2010). Sleep duration as a risk factor for cardiovascular disease- a review of the recent literature. *Current cardiology reviews*, *6*(1), 54-61.

[231] Paruthi, S., Brooks, L. J., D'Ambrosio, C., Hall, W. A., Kotagal, S., Lloyd, R. M., Malow, B. A., Maski, K., Nichols, C., Quan, S. F., Rosen, C. L., Troester, M. M., ... Wise, M. S. (2016). Consensus Statement of the American Academy of Sleep Medicine on the Recommended Amount of Sleep for Healthy Children: Methodology and Discussion. *Journal of clinical sleep medicine : JCSM : official publication of the American Academy of Sleep Medicine, 12*(11), 1549-1561. doi:10.5664/jcsm.6288

[232] Webb WB, Agnew HW. Are we chronically sleep deprived? Bull Psychon Soc. 1975;6:47–8

[233] National Sleep Foundation. Sleep in America Poll 2003.Washington, DC: National Sleep Foundation; 2003

[234] Pickering TG. Could hypertension be a consequence of the 24/7 Society? The effects of sleep deprivation and shift work. J Clin Hypertens (Greenwich) 2006:819–22.

[235] Wolk R, Shamsuzzaman AS, Somers VK. Obesity, sleep apnea, and hypertension. Hypertension. 2003;42:1067–74

[236] Gangwisch JE, Heymsfield SB, Boden-Albala B, et al. Short sleep duration as a risk factor for hypertension. Analyses of the First National Health and Nutrition Examination Survey. Hypertension. 2006;47:833–9

[237] Lusardi P, Mugellini A, Preti P, Zoppi A, Derosa G, Fogani R. Effects of a restricted sleep regimen on ambulatory blood pressure monitoring in normotensive subjects. Am J Hypertens. 1996;9:503–5.

[238] Lusardi P, Zoppi A, Preti P, Pesce RM, Piazza E, Fogari R. Effects of insufficient sleep on ambulatory blood pressure in hypertensive patients: A 24-h study. Am J Hypertens. 1999;12:63–8.

[239] Tochikubo O, Ikeda A, Miyajima E, Ishii M. Effect of insufficient sleep on blood pressure monitored by a new multibiomedical recorder. Hypertension. 1996;27:1318–24.

[240] Zhong X, Hilton HJ, Gates GJ, et al. Increased sympathetic and decreased parasympathetic cardiovascular modulation in normal humans with acute sleep deprivation. J Appl Physiol. 2005;98:2024–2032.

[241] Leung RS, Bradley TD. Sleep apnea and cardiovascular disease. Am J Respir Crit Care Med. 2001;164:2147–65

[242] Ayas NT, White DP, Manson JE, et al. A prospective study of sleep duration and coronary heart disease in women. Arch Intern Med. 2003;163:205–9

[243] Punjabi NM, Polotsky VY. Disorders of glucose metabolism in sleep apnea. J Appl Physiol. 2005;99:1998–2007

[244] Spiegel K, Leproult R, Van Cauter E. Impact of sleep dept on metabolic and endocrine function. Lancet. 1999;354:1435–39

[245] Spiegel K, Knutson K, Leproult R, Tasali E, Van Cauter E. Sleep loss: a novel risk factor for insulin resistance and type 2 diabetes. J Appl Physiol. 2005;99:2008–19.

[246] Spiegel K, Knutson K, Leproult R, Tasali E, Van Cauter E. Sleep loss: a novel risk factor for insulin resistance and type 2 diabetes. J Appl Physiol. 2005;99:2008–19.

[247] Gottlieb DJ, Punjabi NM, Newman AB, et al. Association of sleep time with diabetes mellitus and impaired glucose tolerance. Arch Intern Med. 2005;165:863–7

[248] Yaggi HK, Araujo AB, McKinlay JB. Sleep duration as a risk factor for the development of type 2 diabetes. Diabetes Care. 2006;29:657–61

[249] Leproult R, Copinschi G, Buxton O, Van Cauter E. Sleep loss results in and elevation of cortisol levels the next evening. Sleep. 1997;20:865–70

[250] Wingard DL, Berkman LF. Mortality risk associated sleeping patterns among adults. Sleep. 1983;6:102–7

[251] Kripke DF, Simons RN, Garfinkel L, Hammond EC. Short and long sleep and sleeping pills. Arch Gen Psychiatry. 1979;36:103–16

[252] Gottlieb DJ, Punjabi NM, Newman AB, et al. Association of sleep time with diabetes mellitus and impaired glucose tolerance. Arch Intern Med. 2005;165:863–7

[253] Kalsbeek A, Drijfhout WJ, Westerink BH, et al. GABA receptors in the region of the dorsomedial hypothalamus of rats are implicated in the control of melatonin and corticosterone release. Neuroendocrinology. 1996;63:69–78

[254] Kalsbeek A, Garidou ML, Palm IF, et al. Melatonin sees the light: blocking GABA-ergic transmission in the paraventricular nucleus induces daytime secretion of melatonin. Eur J Neurosci. 2000;12:3146–54

[255] Cui LN, Coderre E, Renaud LP. Glutamate and GABA mediate suprachiasmatic nucleus inputs to spinal-projecting paraventricular neurons. Am J Physiol Regul Integr Comp Physiol. 2001;281:R1283–9

[256] Spiegel K, Leproult R, Van Cauter E. Impact of sleep dept on metabolic and endocrine function. Lancet. 1999;354:1435–39

[257] Leproult R, Copinschi G, Buxton O, Van Cauter E. Sleep loss results in and elevation of cortisol levels the next evening. Sleep. 1997;20:865–70

[258] Luboshitzky R, Zabari Z, Shen-Orr Z, Herer P, Lavie P. Disruption of the nocturnal testosterone rhythm by sleep fragmentation in normal men. J Clin Endocrinol Metab. 2001;86:1134–9.

[259] Barrett-Connor E, Khaw KT. Endogenous sex hormones and cardiovascular disease in men: A prospective population based-study. Circulation. 1988;78:539–45

[260] Haffner SM, Karhapaa P, Mykkanen L, Laakso M. Insulin resistance, body fat distribution, and sex hormones in men. Diabetes. 1994;43:212–9

[261] Simon D, Preziosi P, Barrett-Connor E, et al. Interrelation between plasma testosterone and plasma insulin in healthy adult men: the Telecom Study. Diabetologia. 1992;35:173–7

[262] Stellato RK, Feldman HA, Hamdy O, Horton ES, McKinlay JB. Testosterone, sex hormone-binding globulin, and the development of type 2 diabetes in middle-aged men: prospective results from the Massachusetts Male Aging Study. Diabetes Care. 2000;23:490–4

[263] Haffner SM, Laakso M, Miettinen H, Mykkanen L, Karhapaa P, Rainwater DL. Low levels of sex hormone-binding globulin and testosterone are smaller, denser low density lipoprotein in normoglycemic men. J Clinic Endocrinol Metab. 1996;81:3697–701

[264] Reaven GM, Lithell H, Landsberg L. Hypertenison and associated metabolic abnormalities: the role of insulin resistance and the sympathoadrenal system. N Engl J Med. 1996;334:374–81

[265] Ayas NT, White DP, Manson JE, et al. A prospective study of sleep duration and coronary heart disease in women. Arch Intern Med. 2003;163:205–9

[266] Wolk R, Shamsuzzaman AS, Somers VK. Obesity, sleep apnea, and hypertension. Hypertension. 2003;42:1067–74

[267] Schmid H.A. Decreased Melatonin Biosynthesis, Calcium Flux, Pineal Gland Calcification and Aging: A Hypothetical Framework. Gerontology 1993;39:189 199.

[268] Jennifer Anne Luke. The Effect of Fluoride on the Physiology of the Pineal Gland. Excerpts from pages: 1-9; 51-53; 167-177. 1997.

[269] Zimmerman RA, Bilaniuk LT. Age-related incidence of pineal calcification detected by computed tomography. Radiology. 1982 Mar;142(3):659-62.

[270] National Center for Chronic Disease Prevention and Health Promotion, Division of Population Health | CDC.gov

[271] Mitchell DM1, Henao MP, Finkelstein JS, Burnett-Bowie SA. Prevalence and predictors of vitamin D deficiency in healthy adults. Endocr Pract. 2012 Nov-Dec;18(6):914-23. doi: 10.4158/EP12072.OR.

[272] Ornish Lifestyle Medicine Program, Ornish.com

[273] Mind-body research moves towards the mainstream. *EMBO Rep.* 2006;7(4):358-61.

[274] Simons LE, Elman I, Borsook D. Psychological processing in chronic pain: a neural systems approach. *Neurosci Biobehav Rev.* 2013;39:61–78. doi:10.1016/j.neubiorev.2013.12.006

[275] "Low Back Pain: Relaxation Techniques for Back Pain." *InformedHealth.org [Internet].*, U.S. National Library of Medicine, 14 Feb. 2019, www.ncbi.nlm.nih.gov/books/NBK284952/.

[276] Castelnuovo G, Giusti EM, Manzoni GM, et al. Psychological Treatments and Psychotherapies in the Neurorehabilitation of Pain: Evidences and Recommendations from the Italian Consensus Conference on Pain in Neurorehabilitation. *Front Psychol.* 2016;7:115. Published 2016 Feb 19. doi:10.3389/fpsyg.2016.00115

[277] Braden BB, Pipe TB, Smith R, Glaspy TK, Deatherage BR, Baxter LC. Brain and behavior changes associated with an abbreviated 4-week mindfulness-based stress reduction course in back pain patients. *Brain Behav.* 2016;6(3):e00443. Published 2016 Feb 16. doi:10.1002/brb3.443

[278] Schechter, David, et al. "Outcomes of a Mind-Body Treatment Program for Chronic Back Pain with No Distinct Structural Pathology--a Case Series of Patients Diagnosed and Treated as Tension Myositis Syndrome." *Alternative Therapies in Health and Medicine*, U.S. National Library of Medicine, 2007, www.ncbi.nlm.nih.gov/pubmed/17900039.

[279] Thimmapuram JR, Grim R, Bell T, et al. Factors Influencing Work-Life Balance in Physicians and Advance Practice Clinicians and the Effect of Heartfulness Meditation Conference on Burnout. Glob Adv Health Med. 2019;8:2164956118821056. Published 2019 Jan 15. doi:10.1177/2164956118821056

[280] Pascoe MC, e. (2019). *Yoga, mindfulness-based stress reduction and stress-related physiological measures: A meta-analysis. - PubMed - NCBI.* [online] Ncbi.nlm.nih.gov. Available at: https://www.ncbi.nlm.nih.gov/pubmed/28963884 [Accessed 13 Feb. 2019].

[281] Sharma S, e. (2019). *Development of a yoga module targeting cardiovascular health for patients with post-myocardial left ventricular dysfunction in India. - PubMed - NCBI.* [online] Ncbi.nlm.nih.gov. Available at: https://www.ncbi.nlm.nih.gov/pubmed/30670239 [Accessed 13 Feb. 2019].

[282] Cramer H, e. (2019). *Yoga in Arterial Hypertension. - PubMed - NCBI.* [online] Ncbi.nlm.nih.gov. Available at: https://www.ncbi.nlm.nih.gov/pubmed/30722837 [Accessed 12 Feb. 2019].

[283] Sha K, e. (2019). *Yoga's Biophysiological Effects on Lower Urinary Tract Symptoms: A Scoping Review. - PubMed - NCBI.* [online] Ncbi.nlm.nih.gov. Available at: https://www.ncbi.nlm.nih.gov/pubmed/30735055 [Accessed 12 Feb. 2019].

[284] Pascoe MC, e. (2019). *Mindfulness mediates the physiological markers of stress: Systematic review and meta-analysis. - PubMed - NCBI.* [online] Ncbi.nlm.nih.gov. Available at: https://www.ncbi.nlm.nih.gov/pubmed/28863392 [Accessed 13 Feb. 2019].

[285] Hoge EA, e. (2019). *Effects of mindfulness meditation on occupational functioning and health care utilization in individuals with anxiety. - PubMed - NCBI.* [online] Ncbi.nlm.nih.gov. Available at: https://www.ncbi.nlm.nih.gov/pubmed/28314552 [Accessed 13 Feb. 2019].

[286] J, H. (2019). *Complementary and Integrative Health Practices for Depression. - PubMed - NCBI.* [online] Ncbi.nlm.nih.gov. Available at: https://www.ncbi.nlm.nih.gov/pubmed/28892554 [Accessed 13 Feb. 2019].

[287] NB, S. (2019). *Meditation and mindfulness in clinical practice. - PubMed - NCBI.* [online] Ncbi.nlm.nih.gov. Available at: https://www.ncbi.nlm.nih.gov/pubmed/24975623 [Accessed 13 Feb. 2019].

[288] Cramer H, e. (2019). *Is the practice of yoga or meditation associated with a healthy lifestyle? Results of a national cross-sectional survey of 28,695 Australian women. - PubMed - NCBI.* [online] Ncbi.nlm.nih.gov. Available at: https://www.ncbi.nlm.nih.gov/pubmed/28867414 [Accessed 12 Feb. 2019].

[289] Lardone A, Liparoti M, Sorrentino P, et al. Mindfulness Meditation Is Related to Long-Lasting Changes in Hippocampal Functional Topology during Resting State: A Magnetoencephalography Study. *Neural Plast.* 2018;2018:5340717. Published 2018 Dec 18. doi:10.1155/2018/5340717

[290] KK, D. (2019). Meditation induces physical relaxation and enhances cognition: A perplexing paradox. - PubMed - NCBI. [online] Ncbi.nlm.nih.gov. Available at: https://www.ncbi.nlm.nih.gov/pubmed/30732847 [Accessed 12 Feb. 2019].

[291] Khalsa DS. Stress, Meditation, and Alzheimer's Disease Prevention: Where The Evidence Stands. *J Alzheimers Dis.* 2015;48(1):1-12.

[292] Ornish Lifestyle Medicine Program, Ornish.com

[293] Z, J. (2019). *Love and compassion meditation: a nondual perspective. - PubMed - NCBI.* [online] Ncbi.nlm.nih.gov. Available at: https://www.ncbi.nlm.nih.gov/pubmed/27152716 [Accessed 13 Feb. 2019].

Made in the USA
Columbia, SC
12 December 2024

accb0858-6c19-4934-a0d8-2581c002cda8R01